D1155205

WITHDRAWN

The Structure of
Psychological Common Sense

The Structure of
Psychological Common Sense

Jan Smedslund

LEA LAWRENCE ERLBAUM ASSOCIATES, PUBLISHERS
1997 Mahwah, New Jersey   London

Lawrence Erlbaum Associates, Inc., Publishers
10 Industrial Avenue
Mahwah, New Jersey 07430

Library of Congress Cataloging-in-Publication Data

Smedslund, Jan.
The structure of psychological common sense / Jan
Smedslund.
p. cm.
Includes bibliographical references and index.
ISBN 0-8058-2903-2 (alk. paper)
1. Psychology. I. Title
BF121.S 546 1997
150—DC21   9723186
                                                     CIP

Books published by Lawrence Erlbaum Associates are printed
on acid-free paper and their bindings are chosen for strength
and durability.

Printed in the United States of America
10 9 8 7 6 5 4 3 2 1

Contents

Introduction

How can one work as a psychologist? One encounters one unique and complex person after the other, and the very uniqueness and complexity may seem to preclude practically useful generalizations. Yet something *must* be general if we are to have a psychology at all.

One source of generality can be found in language. The endless diversity of individuals and situations is all the time incorporated into the same schemes, understood by means of the same concepts, described in the same terminology. There seems to be an invariant structure embedded in the way we talk and think about persons, and deal with them. What is this structure and how can it be formulated?

In order to begin to answer this question, we must become more sensitive to word meanings than is usual in contemporary psychology, where language tends to be *invisible*. By this I mean that psychologists tend to focus on the phenomena and procedures under consideration and to use language unreflectively in describing and explaining them. The phenomena and procedures are apprehended in terms of a language, but the language itself is not in focus. It is composed of a multitude of more or less unanalyzed terms and consequently, the meaning of what is stated can be grasped only intuitively. One cannot formally decide what follows and does not follow logically from any given psychological statement and therefore, it is not possible to distinguish between what is noncontingent (necessarily true or necessarily false) and contingent (possibly true and possibly false). Seen from this perspective, unanalyzed language is an obstacle to scientific progress.

Psychologic is a project of explicating the implicit conceptual system of psychology embedded in ordinary language, or in other words, the basic assumptions and distinctions underlying our ways of thinking and talking about psychological phenomena. The first version of psychologic (Smedslund, 1988a) is here referred to as PL, and the present version is called EL (referring to the initial working title of this book, "Elements of Psychologic"). The development of PL, and the subsequent transition from PL to EL has occurred in the context of a continuous critical discussion with other psychologists over a period of altogether two decades. See Appendix D. The arguments and counterarguments are not repeated here. However, I believe it is instructive to consider the outcome of the revision process. In what follows, I compare EL with its predecessor PL, describing how the systems are similar and how they are different, and discussing why this is so.

Stable Content.   Content has remained remarkably unchanged in the transition from PL to EL over a period of 8 years. The content of all the 26 axioms in PL is retained in EL. Twenty two are unchanged or have only minor changes in wording, 3 are condensed into one EL axiom, and one is changed into a theorem. EL has 33 new axioms, but 27 of these are reformulations of definitions in PL, and only 6 are new. The transition from definitions to axioms (see later) has been strictly one way. No axiom in PL has been changed into a definition in EL.

PL contains 83 definitions. EL has retained 32 of these, and added 13 new ones, yielding a total of 45. As already mentioned, 27 of the definitions in PL have become axioms in EL. Finally, 11 of the 22 concepts formally designated as undefined in EL, were defined in PL.

The stability of the content of psychologic, from PL to EL, may be numerically expressed as follows: Of the 109 basic propositions in PL (axioms + definitions), 96 are retained in some form in EL (axioms + primitives + definitions). None of the discarded 13 PL definitions are contradicted in EL. Hence, the two systems are almost identical in content, and appear to reflect a stable kernel structure in psychological common sense.

Although the content is largely unchanged, the form of the propositions involved has changed in three important ways from PL to EL.

Introduction of Undefined Terms.   To explicate (make explicit) means using a language, and using a language means that the meaning of some terms must be taken for granted. We can explicate the meaning of terms by means of other terms, and the meaning of these other terms by means of still other terms, but the process is open-ended and must come to a stop. Hence, the explication of implicit psychology must, ultimately, rely on a set of terms whose meaning is taken for granted. It is also obvious that these terms must come from ordinary language. My selection of undefined concepts has been largely a matter of intuitive judgment, but I have also been inspired by Wierzbicka's work on a natural semantic metalanguage (Goddard & Wierzbicka, 1994), and many of the selected terms are in that language. The undefined terms function as basic elements. They must be evaluated by their potential for being combined into useful definitions and axioms.

The selection of undefined concepts is only in its beginning. PL has not formally designated such terms, and the propositions in EL still contain many terms which are neither defined nor formally designated as undefined. A list of the 22 undefined terms so far selected can be found in Appendix A.

Revised View of the Function of Definitions.   I now think that definitions of ordinary language terms are relatively useless. To define a term such as "sad," for example, is to stipulate what is to be the entire meaning of the term. The contrast between an attempted strict definition of a term and the richness, vagueness, and variability of its meaning in ordinary language leads to repeated and unending debates. See, for example, my proposal of a definition of "sadness" (Smedslund, 1991c), and the commentaries by Cushman (1991), Ossorio (1991), Rosenhan (1991), Shweder (1991), and Williams (1991). There are numerous similar debates about other terms I have tried to define. People already know what the word "sad" means in given contexts, and they argue that no definition can catch this subtle knowledge in a totally satisfactory way. If this is accepted and generalized to other ordinary language terms, the only proper use of definitions in psychological theory appears to lie in the introduction of *technical/scientific* terms. These do not belong to ordinary language and hence, need to be explicitly introduced and explained to the reader. They can be construed in precise, context-independent and, hence, definable ways. The definitions that remain in EL are all of this type. They are listed in Appendix B.

From Definitions to Axioms   The difficulty of formulating satisfactory definitions of ordinary language terms does not mean that the domain is entirely chaotic. Proposed definitions do catch something important, even though they cannot cover the full meaning of the terms. In my view, axioms can take over the role of definitions in providing a foundation for a deductive system. Briefly, the argument goes as follows: A definition stipulates exactly what a term shall mean and hence, exhausts and fixates its semantic content ("X shall mean exactly the same as Y"). On the other hand, an axiom stipulates that the term shall have a fixed relation to one or a few other terms, but except for this, leaves its meaning open (X, if, and only if, Y). Hence, moving from definition to axiom means moving from freezing the total meaning of a term to freezing its relation to one other term only. As already mentioned, this has taken place to a considerable extent in the development of psychologic from PL to EL.

The preceding means that axioms are becoming the most important basic premises for EL as a formal deductive system. They attempt to catch the core or essence of the meanings of terms.

Elimination of Reference to Context and Time.   The clause "in C at t," used in PL, is eliminated from all formulae in EL. The clause was originally introduced in order to safeguard the propositions. Statements referring to the same moment in time and the same context were intended to ensure conservation of the constituent elements and hence, the applicability of logic. If one premise refers to one time and/or one context and another premise to another time and/or another context, the validity of a logical inference becomes uncertain and depends on nothing relevant having changed or nothing relevant being different. For example, if A > B and B > C, the validity of the logical conclusion A > C depends on the assumption of conservation over time of A, B, and C. If one of the quantities has increased or decreased between the recording of A > B, B > C, and the final comparison of A and C, then the standard conclusion A > C may be wrong.

The argument for eliminating "in C at t" is that it is, after all, unnecessary. Although instantiations of logic always refer to a given time and a given context, logical structure itself is valid irrespective of time and place. A logical structure implicitly presupposes that premises are unchanged and therefore, does not need to be explicitly safeguarded by the clause "in C at t." The elimination of the clause also abbreviates the formulae and hence, increases their elegance.

Avoidance of Metatheory. PL contains an extensive metatheoretical discussion, and was preceded and succeeded by metatheoretical debates. (See the references in Appendix D.) Here I avoid this. EL is presented without discussing its metatheoretical status. I have come to believe that prolonged such discussion may be relatively unprofitable. Determination of the value of EL can take place through evaluating the logical consistency, predictive power, and practical usefulness of the system. In this respect, psychologic is not different from, for example, Euclidean geometry or Newtonian mechanics. These systems work within certain ranges of application. The same may be true for psychologic. If it does work then it is useful, even though one has not yet reached an agreement, for example, about the empirical or a priori nature of the axioms.

The system presented here is composed of what Lewis (1972) labeled "platitudes" of folk psychology. The reader is invited to consider carefully the meaning and implications of these "platitudes." Each of them is set forth as an exceptionless generalization with predictive value in everyday life, as well as in the psychological laboratory and consulting room. The system is supposed to function as a calculus by means of which psychological processes can be explained, predicted, and controlled. It is my contention that it is the only way in which this can be done.

Acknowledgments

Ever since the publication of *Psycho-Logic* in 1988, I have worked on revising and improving the system. Now that that book has gone out of print, it is time to bring out a new version. A main source of inspiration has been the discussions over the past 3 years with Tore Helstrup and our students in the seminar "Theoretical Problems in Psychology," and also with Waldemar Rognes.

The Research Council of Norway has supported the publication of this book.

I am grateful to the Department of Psychology, Stanford University, and the Department of Psychology, University of New Mexico, for allowing me to work undisturbed as visiting scholar for 2 and 4 months respectively, in the first half of 1993. For the remainder of the period, the Institute of Psychology in Oslo has been a familiar and protective setting for my work. The daily luncheon has continued to offer stimulating intellectual exchanges in a warm atmosphere.

Working with clients has served as a constant reminder of the complexity of the human realities that the book is about.

Finally, I want to thank my wife, Åsebrit Sundquist, for loving and intellectual companionship.

—Jan Smedslund

Chapter 1

Persons

Note 1.0.0 *Persons* are individuals of the species Homo sapiens and can be regarded as natural entities. *Psychology* is the study of persons.

Primitive term 1.0.1 *Person*

Note 1.0.2 Persons are highly distinct entities just as organisms are. Although, normally, one person corresponds to one human organism, the phenomena of *multiple personalities* highlight the fact that an organism and a person are quite different concepts. In rare cases, two or more persons can be clearly distinguished, even though they are manifested by the same organism.

Note 1.0.3 Because psychologists study persons, and because psychologists themselves are persons, *personal encounter* is involved in every instance of psychological research and practice. Major parts of the present work consist of analyses of the preconditions, concomitants, and outcomes of personal encounters.

Note 1.0.4 When we encounter a person, numerous conceptual schemes are engaged. This chapter presents five of these dichotomous schemes, namely *subjective/objective*, *intentional/causal*, *normative/neutral*, *reflective/unreflective*, and *reversible/irreversible*. Person processes are always subjective, intentional, and normative, and they may be either reflective or unreflective, and reversible or irreversible.

1.1 *The Subjective*

Primitive term 1.1.0 *Aware*

Note 1.1.1 In encountering a person, we take it for granted that the person is aware of what goes on, that is, that the world exists *for* the person. We also take it for granted that the person's awareness is limited, that is, refers to only *some* of the indefinitely numerous parts, aspects, and possibilities of the world. The limits are both internal (limited capacities) and external (limited availability of information, given previous history and current situation). Because different persons have different capacities, different histories, and different current situations, what exists for them (their subjective worlds) also differs. Getting to know a person entails getting to know what exists for that person.

Note 1.1.2 What exists for a person includes not only everything the person can report, but also everything the person automatically presupposes or takes for granted. These presuppositions exist *for* the person and are built into his or her experience and acting. However, although they are subjective, the person may not be aware of *that* he or she has them. Hence, what exists for a person at a given moment is much more than what the person is aware *that* he or she is aware of at that moment. In order to make it explicit that awareness, as used in psychologic, refers to the entire subjective world, the following axiom is proposed (P is a person, X is anything):

Axiom 1.1.3 *P is aware of X, if, and only if, X exists FOR P.*

Note 1.1.4 Axiom 1.1.3 explicates part of the meaning of "P is aware of X," namely that it is equivalent to "X exists for P." One can determine what exists *for* P even in cases where P is not aware *that* P is aware of something. Example: A person always began to smile when the social situation got tense, and ceased to smile when the situation became easier. This was regularly observed by friends of the person, and one of them said: "Why do you always smile when people are angry?" The person became very surprised, but had to admit that it was true. Her automatic smiling showed that she had been aware of changes in the social situation, even though she did not realize *that* she was aware of them and *that* she responded to them in the way she did.

Note 1.1.5 In the preceding example, and in psychology in general, one must acknowledge the existence of three kinds of reality, namely the *subjective*, the *social*, and the *material* realities. The situation as it existed for the smiling person was her subjective reality, the aspects of the situation shared by the participants was the social reality, and the physical objects and events involved made up the material reality.

Definition 1.1.6 *"Subjective reality of a person"* = df *"What exists FOR that person."* "= df " means "is by definition equal to".

Definition 1.1.7 *"Social reality of a community"* = df *"What everyone in that community takes for granted, **and** everyone takes for granted that everyone takes for granted, **and** everyone takes for granted that everyone takes for granted that everyone takes for granted."*

Definition 1.1.8 *"Material reality"* = df *"What exists independently of persons."*

Note 1.1.9 What exists *for* a person, may or may not correspond to anything in the social or the material reality. Also, what exists in the social reality may or may not correspond to anything in the material reality and vice versa. Finally, a person may or may not be correct in his or her judgments of another person's subjective reality or of given social and/or material realities.

Note 1.1.10 According to Definition 1.1.7, even if something is taken for granted by all members of a community it need not be a part of social reality. It becomes social reality only when, and to the extent that, everyone also takes it for granted that everyone else takes it for granted, and that everyone takes it for granted that everyone else takes it for granted that everyone else takes it for granted. Time and location of events are examples of social reality.

Note 1.1.11 The mode of existing *for* someone defines a domain clearly different from that of natural science, which involves events and objects taken to exist independently of persons. The dependence of awareness *on* someone is a *logical* relation. Something cannot be said to exist *for*, if there is no one for whom it exists. On the other hand, phenomena which exist independently of someone continue to exist even if that someone ceases to exist.

Note 1.1.12 The assumption that someone is a person, hence, entails that a world exists *for* that someone. It makes no sense to think of a person for whom nothing ever exists. But, although awareness, in the sense of existence for, is a necessary characteristic of a person, it is not a sufficient one. Animals are also aware, but are not persons. Important distinguishing features of persons are described under the headings of normativity and reflectivity.

Note 1.1.13 Although a person must be capable of becoming aware of something, it is not the case that the person is always capable of this. In deep sleep, and under sedation, a person is not aware of anything. The concept of consciousness is needed to differentiate between states of a person with respect to capacity for awareness.

Axiom 1.1.14 *P is conscious if, and only if, P is in a state in which P is aware of something.*

Corollary 1.1.15 *If P is not aware of anything, then P is not conscious.*
Proof: This follows directly from Axiom 1.1.14.

Corollary 1.1.16 *If P is aware of something, then P is conscious.*   Proof: This follows directly from Axiom 1.1.14.

Corollary 1.1.17 *If P is conscious, then P is aware of something.*   Proof: This follows directly from Axiom 1.1.14.

Note 1.1.18 The fruitfulness of the dispositional concept of consciousness, as defined here, lies in that if P is aware of something, then P can usually become aware of other things normally accessible to P's awareness. Conversely, if P cannot become aware of something normally accessible to P's awareness, then P may be expected not to become aware of other things, also normally accessible to P's awareness. In other words, if P responds normally to an ordinary event, then P can be expected to respond normally to other ordinary events, and if P does not respond normally to an ordinary event, then P can be expected not to respond normally to other ordinary events.

Note 1.1.19 One may distinguish between *degrees* of being conscious, from being fully conscious to being fully unconscious.There are also the specific distinctions between being asleep and being awake, between different depths of sleep, different degrees of sleepiness, and between being asleep and being unconscious because of a physical trauma or chemical agent. The sleeper can be awakened and the person in coma cannot. In what follows, these distinctions are not being further considered, and all persons are simply taken to be fully conscious. This entails that they are continuously aware, that is, that a world continuously exists *for* them.

Note 1.1.20 The distinction emphasized in the preceding discussion of subjectivity is between what exists *for* a person and what does *not* exist for a person. This distinction leads to usage of the terms aware and conscious that on some occasions differs from ordinary usage. Awareness of something here means that something exists for a person, whereas consciousness here refers to a state in which a person can be aware of things. Hence, it does not make sense in the present terminology to talk about psychological processes of which a person is unaware, because awareness is precisely the defining criterion of a psychological process. Later, I introduce another relevant distinction, namely reflective versus unreflective awareness, the latter referring to what in many psychological theories are called "unconscious" processes.

Note 1.1.21 A person's subjectivity is not something that can be observed but is something *encountered*. There is an unavoidable mutuality in encounter. I see (hear) you, I see (hear) you seeing (hearing) me, I see (hear) you seeing (hearing) me seeing (hearing) you, and so on. Hence, persons encounter not only material and social reality, but also the other person's unique subjectivity. There is always *commonality* in an encounter. Unless two persons share a sufficient number of presuppositions about meaning, they cannot get to know each other's subjective worlds. In research, the participant must correctly understand the meaning of the instruction and the researcher must correctly understand how the participant has understood this meaning. Subjectivity requires a unique methodology.

Note 1.1.22 We cannot avoid the category of subjectivity. We cannot live our lives regarding ourselves and our fellow human beings as merely objective, material entities. Similarly, we cannot avoid the category of social reality. On a given occasion, it really *is* New Years Eve, and this is a fact independent both of physical measurement and of individual subjective opinion.

1.2 *The Intentional*

Note 1.2.0 Persons are continuously active, and all languages have numerous terms for these activities. This topic is treated in detail in chapter 2. Here, one salient aspect of personal activity is discussed, namely its intentionality.

Primitive term 1.2.1 *Act (Do)*

Note 1.2.2 In encountering a person we take it for granted that the person acts, does things, or expresses him or herself, *in order to* reach goals, looks and listens *in order to* determine what is going on, and so on. The person is continuously sensitive to the outcome of these activities, which means adjusting subsequent activities in the light of what resulted from earlier ones. This characteristic of acting is labeled *intentionality.*

Definition 1.2.3 *"Intentional"* = df *"directed by a preference for achieving a goal."*

Axiom 1.2.4 *Acting is intentional.*

Corollary 1.2.5 *Acting is directed by a preference for achieving a goal.*
Proof: This follows directly from Definition 1.2.3 and Axiom 1.2.4.

Corollary 1.2.6 *If P does something not directed by a preference for achieving a goal, then what P does is not acting.* Proof: This follows directly from Definition 1.2.3 and Axiom 1.2.4.

Note 1.2.7 The present terminology deviates from certain usages in ordinary language. In that language, something is said to be done "intentionally," only when it is preceded by an "intention" or "decision" to act. Here, intentional activity refers to all activity that involves preference for achieving a goal, and that, consequently, is sensitive to outcomes. No preceding and separate intention or decision is required. Coughing is an act to the extent that it is sensitive to outcome, for example, ceases when it is met with reproachful stares from members of the audience at a concert. On the other hand, coughing is not an act to the extent that it continues unaffected by these outcomes. Similarly, the shaking of a person's hand due to Parkinson's disease is not an act, because outcome has no influence. The hand continues to shake and spill coffee, irrespective of the consequences.

Definition 1.2.8 *"X is relevant for achieving a goal G"* = df *"taking X into account increases the likelihood of achieving G."*

Corollary 1.2.9 *If P believes that X is relevant for achieving G, then P believes that taking X into account increases the likelihood of achieving G.*
Proof: This follows directly from Definition 1.2.8.

Theorem 1.2.10 *P takes into account what P takes to be relevant for the achievement of P's goal.* Proof: According to Corollary 1.2.5, activity is directed by a preference for achieving a goal. Therefore, activity is directed by a preference for doing whatever is taken to increase the likelihood of achieving the goal. According to Definition 1.2.8, this likelihood increases by taking into account what is relevant for the achievement of the goal. From this the theorem follows.

Corollary 1.2.11 *If P is aware of X1, and P takes X1 to be relevant for achieving P's goal X2, then P takes X1 into account in attempting to achieve X2.* Proof: This follows directly from Theorem 1.2.10.

Theorem 1.2.12 *P avoids what P takes to be an obstacle to the achievement of P's goal.* Proof: It follows from Corollary 1.2.5 that P's acting is directed by a preference for achieving a goal. A preference for achieving a goal implies a preference for doing what increases the likelihood of achieving the goal and avoiding what decreases that likelihood. But, something that is taken to be an obstacle to the achievement of a goal, decreases the likelihood of achieving the goal. Therefore, it is avoided.

Note 1.2.13 Because, according to Axiom 1.2.4, action is intentional, apparent nonintentional activity, must always be reinterpreted in ways which uphold intentionality: The very occurrence of a specific activity, instead of all the others that could have occurred, can always be taken to indicate a preference. Conversely, if an activity is clearly not sensitive to outcome and hence, is nonintentional, it must be interpreted as something other than an act (e.g., uncontrollable coughing or shaking). This was formally stated in Corollary 1.2.6. Intentionality is a conceptual scheme that we cannot avoid.

Note 1.2.14 Doing something for its own sake (intrinsic motivation) also fits the intentional scheme. Attempts to stop a person from engaging in a desired activity for its own sake lead to attempts to circumvent the obstacles, and successful engagement in the activity leads to future attempts to repeat it.

Note 1.2.15 The preceding propositions do not allow for people making errors, forgetting things, and overlooking things. It is assumed that everything that is taken to be relevant, and only that, is always taken into account in attempts to achieve goals. This assumption is here given the status of an axiom, but is slightly weakened.

Axiom 1.2.16 *A person's acting tends to be completely integrated (unitary).*

Note 1.2.17 Persons do not always perform with machine-like perfection. Therefore, Axiom 1.2.16 contains the expression "tends to." This acknowledges the occurrence of errors and inconsistencies, while at the same time upholding the general rule. In everyday life, propositions such as Corollary 1.2.9, Theorem 1.2.10, Corollary 1.2.11 and Theorem 1.2.12, are generally relied on, even though exceptions to them are acknowledged to occur.

Note 1.2.18 In the scheme of intentionality, the concept of *context* (C) has an important place. Everything a person experiences, or does, has surrounding circumstances which influence the experiences and acts, and what they mean to the person. Personal processes never occur in isolation, but always are parts of larger structured wholes.

Definition 1.2.19 *"The context of an act A of P"* = df *"The set of everything P is aware of and takes to be relevant for attaining the goal of A."*

Note 1.2.20 Acts often have exceedingly complex contexts, in which the parts tend to be mutually dependent. The determination of contexts is a major practical problem in psychology. Everything that, if changed, makes a difference for a person's act A, is a part of the context for that person doing A. This can be given status as a theorem.

Theorem 1.2.21 *If a change in X leads to a change in P's act A, then X is a part of the context of A.* Proof: If a change in X leads to a change in P's act A, then, P is aware of X and takes X into account as relevant for achieving the goal of A. From this it follows, according to Definition 1.2.19, that X is a part of the context of A.

Note 1.2.22 Contextual elements may belong to the past, the present, and/or the future. A person acts taking for granted certain things about what happened earlier, about the present state of affairs, and about what is expected or planned to happen in the future. Common to them is that acting changes with changes in these elements.

Note 1.2.23 The scheme of intentionality is deeply ingrained in how we think about psychology. Our daily lives are predicated on this way of looking at acting. It follows that the formal propositions presented are indispensable also in the project of psychologic.

1.3 *The Normative*

Primitive term 1.3.0 *Right*

Primitive term 1.3.1 *Wrong*

Note 1.3.2 When encountering a person, the need to treat that person correctly and properly always arises. It is taken for granted that the person will be sensitive to this. Likewise, you are sensitive to how the person treats you. There are rules for what is considered to be polite, considerate, and just, and these must be adhered to in order to ensure continued and orderly contact. In addition to the rules regulating how persons are to be treated (ethical rules), there are innumerable rules regulating how things are done and said. For example, language consists of rules for how words are spelled, how words are combined, what words mean, and so on. Breaking these rules will elicit corrections from others. The normative aspect is present at every moment and in every detail of every personal encounter.

Note 1.3.3 It is a central aspect of social life that almost everything a person does has potential consequences for the surrounding other persons, and that almost everything the surrounding other persons do has potential consequences for the person. This vulnerability of people to the acts of others (Axiom 5.5.2) necessitates a regulating rule that can be expressed in the following axiom:

Axiom 1.3.4 *A person is held responsible for his or her acts by everyone involved.*

Note 1.3.5 The responsibility is generally upheld both by the actor and by the others. It means that the person must be given and must accept rewards and punishments for past acts. Because the record of one's past acts is important, the future also becomes so. You will be held responsible in the future for what you do now, which will then be in the past. This ever-present responsibility discourages individuals from living in the present.

Note 1.3.6 A person is held *accountable* for his or her acts, which means that the person is expected to be able to describe and explain what he or she has done in acceptable ways. The person is held responsible for these descriptions and explanations too. To account for one's actions requires reflective awareness and ability to talk. As children grow older they are held increasingly accountable for their actions, and, hence, are pressured to reflect and talk about what they have done.

Note 1.3.7 If a person is unable to account for his or her actions, he or she is often not held to be responsible for them. The person may, because of this, be partially or wholly deprived of his or her status as complete person, at least in that context.

Note 1.3.8 Responsibility refers to the *rules* governing interaction. These rules determine what is *right* and *wrong* in the given community. In order for a community to function, the participating persons must, normally, follow the rules and, hence, treat each other rightly, and proceed correctly. The following two axioms are taken to be valid for all persons:

Axiom 1.3.9 *P wants to do what P believes is right, and wants not to do what P believes is wrong.*

Note 1.3.10 It is not asserted that a person will always and necessarily act rightly. This also depends on the strength of the person's *other* beliefs and wants in the given situation at the given time, as well as on what the person actually *can* do and *believes* he or she can do. However, the axiom asserts that a normative belief is always accompanied by a normative want.

Axiom 1.3.11 *P wants everyone to accept what P believes is right and to reject what P believes is wrong.*

Note 1.3.12 Normative beliefs are taken to be valid for everyone. This also means that it is taken to be right for every person, unless higher order beliefs contradict it, to try to persuade others and to enforce rules. Axiom 1.3.11 does not preclude recognition of differences in normative thinking. Example: "I think slavery is wrong, but I recognize that they regard it as right." However, the axiom assumes that if one believes slavery is wrong, then there will be a want to have everyone agree with this.

Note 1.3.13 Subjectivity and intentionality are features that persons share with animals. However, normativity would seem to be an exclusively human characteristic. A demonstration of normativity presupposes some way of distinguishing between a personal preference and a normatively based preference. A killer dog refrains from biting a visitor. What would be a sufficient proof that it refrains from biting in this situation, not because it does not at that moment want to bite, but because it regards this as impolite or otherwise improper? I think no such proof can be convincing because the dog cannot *talk* or in some other way communicate *about* the reasons for its choices. (See the discussion of reflectivity in the next section.)

1.4 *The Unreflective and the Reflective*

Note 1.4.0 Being a person entails being subjective, intentional, and normative. Next, let us consider a feature that, in the same way as normativity, is lacking in animals, but is present in everyone we call a person. This is the ability to *reflect* or to be *reflectively aware*, which has to be distinguished from being *unreflectively aware*.

Definition 1.4.1 "*P is unreflectively aware of X*" = df "*P is aware of X, but P is not aware THAT P is aware of X.*"

Definition 1.4.2 "*P is reflectively aware of X*" = df "*P is aware THAT P is aware of X.*"

Note 1.4.3 The division of awareness into unreflective and reflective is exhaustive and exclusive. If P is aware of X, then P is either unreflectively or reflectively aware of X, but not both.

Note 1.4.4 Two examples of unreflective awareness: The first one is the performance of a person riding a bicycle. The person must be unreflectively aware of each of the departures from equilibrium, because they are rapidly and unerringly compensated for by appropriate movements. However, the person is not aware *that* he or she is aware of these deviations. Another example is the already mentioned case of a person who always began to smile when the social situation became difficult. The smile invariably disappeared when the situation became easier. One may infer that the person was unreflectively aware of the variations in the difficulty of the situation, since the intensity of the soothing smile covaried with these variations. However, there were no indications that the person was aware *that* she smiled or *that* she was aware of the difficulty of the situations. When told about it, she was very surprised, and said that she had not known *that* she smiled.

Note 1.4.5 Reflective awareness is a second-order awareness of a first-order awareness. Sometimes, there is also a third-order awareness that may be called *metareflective awareness*. Examples: (a) Toying with a stick, without being aware that one is doing it. This is unreflective awareness that cannot be talked about, and that is revealed only by what the person does; (b) "I am aware that I am toying with a stick" (reflective awareness), and (c) "I am aware that I am aware that I am toying with a stick" (metareflective awareness). Reflection appears to involve an indefinite regress. Once you are able to reflect, you are also able to reflect on your reflection, and so on. However, the regress is almost always limited to one or two steps.

Axiom 1.4.6 *P can be reflectively aware, if, and only if, P is a person.*

Corollary 1.4.7 *If P can be reflectively aware, then P is a person.*
Proof: This follows directly from Axiom 1.4.6.

Corollary 1.4.8 *If P is a person, then P can be reflectively aware*
Proof: This follows directly from Axiom 1.4.6.

Note 1.4.9 Axiom 1.4.6 characterizes persons by their capacity for reflection. However, this does not preclude decision problems. Is a newborn baby a person? Is a severely mentally deficient individual a person? Some decision problems may stem from lack of sufficient information and some may stem from lack of conceptual clarity. For example, decisions may depend on whether or not it is permissible to speak about *degrees* of being reflectively aware and *degrees* of acting reflectively. If it is permissible to talk about degrees in these cases, then it is also permissible to talk about degrees of being a person. What is important at this point is to remember that Axiom 1.4.6 is a part of the system of psychologic. It is not intended to solve ethical or legal problems and it differs from a wider concept of human being that may include unborn and newborn babies, as well as advanced Alzheimer patients, and permanently unconscious individuals.

Primitive term 1.4.10 *Talk (Say)*

Axiom 1.4.11 *P can talk about what P is reflectively aware of, and only that.*

Note 1.4.12 Axiom 1.4.11 stipulates that there is a complete correspondence between reflective awareness and the use of language. It says nothing about how to understand this correspondence. The use of language to describe something implies a distinction between what is described and the description itself. It also involves reflectivity, because one can always talk about what one has talked about, and so on.

The only way to decide whether or not someone is reflectively aware is through language, either by using language or by somehow responding to language: One may listen to the person talk, or observe the person respond in some way to others talking. Reflective awareness probably is a direct and necessary consequence of the acquisition of language. In talking about what they are aware of, persons, by necessity display reflective awareness.

Corollary 1.4.13 *If P is reflectively aware of X, then P can talk about X.*
Proof: This follows directly from Axiom 1.4.11.

Corollary 1.4.14 *If P can talk about X, then P is reflectively aware of X.*
Proof: This follows directly from Axiom 1.4.11.

Note 1.4.15. In practice, Corollary 1.4.14 is often used to determine whether or not there is reflective awareness of something. If there are no signs of reflective awareness, that is, no relevant talk, the possible existence of unreflective awareness of X may be established by observing if the person consistently acts as if X were the case.

Theorem 1.4.16 *If P can talk, then P is a person.* Proof: It follows from Axiom 1.4.11 that if P can talk about X, then P can be reflectively aware of X. But, according to Corollary 1.4.7, if P can be reflectively aware, then P is a person, and, hence, the theorem follows.

Note 1.4.17 It has *not* been asserted that if P is a person, then P can talk. There are persons who cannot talk. However, if instead of talking one uses the criterion of "using a language," then it would be true that if P is a person, then P can use a language. This could, for example, be the sign language of a deaf mute.

Note 1.4.18 Axiom 1.4.6 serves to distinguish persons from animals. Animals do not seem to be aware *that* they are aware and *that* they act.

Note 1.4.19 Awareness entails the existence of someone who is aware of something. Hence, being aware *of* being aware (reflective awareness) means being aware also of the one who is aware, namely oneself. It follows that every person can be aware of him or herself.

Theorem 1.4.20 *Every person can be aware of him or herself.* Proof: According to Axiom 1.4.6, every person can be reflectively aware. According to Definition 1.4.2, "P is reflectively aware of X" means "P is aware that P is aware of X." But, if P is aware that P is aware of X, then P is also aware of P, as the one who is aware of X. Hence, the theorem is proved.

Note 1.4.21 One may, in principle, distinguish between at least three main categories of unreflective awareness. First, there are all the things we do unreflectively, which we can reflect on when this becomes necessary. For example, how exactly do you brush your teeth? The case of automatic smiling (Notes 1.1.4 and 1.4.4) also illustrates how something unreflective becomes reflective.

Second, P may not be reflectively aware of X, because of its complexity. Many motor performances and social performances require such subtle and rapid adjustments that reflection cannot do justice to them, and may even have a destructive effect. Examples are riding a bike or making conversation.

A third possible category of unreflective awareness refers to when P, unreflectively, wants *not* to become reflectively aware of X, because this is, unreflectively, taken to be intolerably painful. Example: A person is attracted to another person of the same sex. To become reflectively aware of this is very frightening to this person and, hence, the attraction remains unreflective and may only be revealed indirectly in aspects of the person's acting. This conceptually highly problematic third alternative is usually called *repression*.

Definition 1.4.22 *"P is acting reflectively"* = df *"P is aware that P is acting in this way."*

Corollary 1.4.23 *If P is acting reflectively, then P is aware that P is acting in this way.*   Proof: This follows directly from Definition 1.4.22.

Definition 1.4.24 *"P is acting unreflectively"* = df *"P is not aware that P is acting in this way."*

Corollary 1.4.25 *If P is acting unreflectively, then P is not aware that P is acting in this way.*   Proof: This follows directly from Definition 1.4.24.

Note 1.4.26 The difficulty of the idea of unreflective acting stems from the fact that we can talk only about what we are reflectively aware of. What we do unreflectively and do *not* contemplate reflectively, remains unrecognized and undescribed. Therefore, we, ordinarily, are able to live with the impression that we are aware of everything we are doing. Recognition of the limitations of reflective awareness often comes from what others tell us about ourselves, or from contemplating the activity of others. Occasionally, we may come across traces of our own activity, which show that we must have done things without being aware that we did it. The piece of soap is in the refrigerator, so I must have put it there, while being absorbed in something else.

Note 1.4.27 A person who says "X" can almost always, immediately afterward, say "I said 'X'," and talk about that. Similarly, an attentive listener to a person who says "X" can almost always, immediately afterward, say "P said 'X'," and talk about that. Both listening to oneself talk and listening to others talk appear to involve reflective awareness. A talker and a listener can almost always talk about what was just said. In fact this may be seen as an integral part of being able to use a language.

Theorem 1.4.28 *Listening to talk involves reflective awareness.*   Proof: Listening to talk means being aware of what the talk is about, and being able to talk about that. But, according to Axiom 1.4.11, one can talk about what one is reflectively aware of, and only that. Therefore, listening must involve reflective awareness too.

Note 1.4.29 Unreflective awareness has belief-character, in the sense that what is apprehended always *refers to* or *means* something. Hence, it is always subject to possible error. On the other hand, P's reflective awareness *of* his or her unreflective awareness is infallible. While P's seeing an oasis may be an illusion, P cannot be mistaken in being aware *that* P is seeing an oasis.

Note 1.4.30 Unreflective awareness has want-character, in the sense that what is apprehended always has some *value* (is more or less wanted). Hence, it is always subject to possible error. The delicious looking apple that makes your mouth water may turn out to be unpalatable. On the other hand, P's reflective awareness *of* P's unreflective want of an apple is infallible. While P's wanting to have something may be a mistake, P may not be mistaken about wanting that something.

Note 1.4.31 A person may lie in describing an experience, or distort the description. However, if the person is honest and regards his or her description as adequate, then the description is the ultimate criterion of what the person is reflectively aware of. This is expressed in the following axiom.

Axiom 1.4.32 *P's description of what P is reflectively aware of is correct, to the extent that P regards it as correct.*

Note 1.4.33 Reflective awareness also has belief- and want-character and, hence, does not represent some kind of neutral mirror of the unreflective awareness. Two examples will suffice: A person perceives a stick half submerged in water as broken. The reflective awareness of this impression may be that it is an illusion. In this case, there is a conflict between the unreflective and the reflective level about what is the case. Another example: A person unreflectively wants to take another drink. Reflectively, the person wants to stop drinking. Again, there is a conflict between the two levels of awareness, this time about what should be done.

Note 1.4.34 Preferences involve taking more or less inclusive contexts into account. Of particular importance is the distinction between long-term and short-term consequences of a choice. Unreflective action takes into account only the here-and-now, whereas reflective action includes a consideration of talked about long-term consequences. This can be formalized as follows:

Corollary 1.4.35 *Only reflective awareness can take long-term consequences into account.*   Proof: Long-term consequences are not present and, hence, cannot be directly apprehended, but only talked about. According to Axiom 1.4.11, P can talk about what P is reflectively aware of, and only that. Hence, taking long-term consequences into account must involve reflective awareness.

Corollary 1.4.36 *Unreflective awareness cannot take long-term consequences into account.*   Proof: This follows directly from Definitions 1.4.1 and 1.4.2 and Corollary 1.4.35.

Note 1.4.37 Among the implications of the preceding is that reflective action can take into account any contexts referred to by talk. One may include in this the person talking to him or herself. On the other hand, unreflective action takes into account only the here-and-now situation. The prototype for this is, of course, animal behavior. One specific implication is that the reflective human actor can, sometimes, defer gratification by talking to him or herself about long-term consequences, whereas, the unreflective human actor may succumb to immediately present temptations.

Note 1.4.38 Another aspect of reflectivity, and of being able to talk about something, is that it entails being aware of one's having a *viewpoint*, and of the existence of alternative perspectives. Unreflective awareness does not distinguish between different perspectives. This must be stated as an axiom:

> **Axiom 1.4.39** *The unreflective is not differentiated according to viewpoints.*

> **Corollary 1.4.40** *P's unreflective awareness does not involve awareness of a viewpoint.*   Proof: This follows directly from Axiom 1.4.39.

Note 1.4.41 Because unreflective awareness is subjective and exists for the holder, it does, in fact, involve a viewpoint. However, this viewpoint does not exist for the bearer. If I, unreflectively, take it for granted that I am inferior, there is no awareness that it is I who takes this for granted, and that there may be other viewpoints. Only with reflection comes the possibility of recognizing subjectivity.

Note 1.4.42 Psychotic states may involve unreflective functioning. For example, a client of mine, who had been through several psychotic episodes made the following retrospective observations: (a) "I experienced that everyone shared my point of view. There was only one point of view"; (b) "I experienced that everything had meaning directly accessible to me"; (c) "I had no experience of being in a particular state. I could not reflect"; and (d) "Even the simplest everyday tasks appeared to be overwhelmingly difficult."

Note 1.4.43 Personal processes have so far been characterized as subjective, intentional, normative, and reflective or unreflective. The next step is to consider the irreversibility and reversibility of these processes.

1.5 *The Irreversible and the Reversible.*

Note 1.5.0 When two persons meet we take it for granted that what happens early on in the encounter will influence what will take place later on, and that the participants are changing in some ways as they get to know each other. This process is *irreversible* in the sense that it cannot be strictly undone. Once we have come to recognize the face of a person, there is no direct way of making us *not* recognize that face, and so on.

Note 1.5.1 What is true of personal encounters is also true of the entire lives of persons. Each person is a product of a preceding life history and a participant in a continuing such history. Other ways of phrasing this are to say that people *learn from experience*, or that they *remember* what happens to them. If a person comes to recognize a difference between two things (discrimination) or becomes able to distinguish in actual performance between two ways of acting (differentiation) there is no direct way of making the person become unaware of these differences again. One cannot undiscriminate and undifferentiate. Similarly, if a person comes to understand what something means, for example, in a foreign language or culture, the person cannot obliterate that understanding. Finally, the same is true for all learning of what follows what or what leads to what. One cannot return to the initial state of expectancy.

In some cases, it may, at first sight, appear that one *can* unlearn. For example, one may first learn that A leads to B, and then learn that A no longer leads to B. Finally, one may again learn that A leads to B. However, even in such cases, there is never a complete return to the original state. The latest belief that A leads to B differs from the original one in that it has the preceding changes as a context.

The preceding may be generalized in the following axiom:

Axiom 1.5.2 *Learning (the impact of experience) is irreversible.*

Note 1.5.3 The impact of experience referred to in axiom 1.5.2 covers learning to discriminate, to differentiate, to understand, and what follows what, and what leads to what. The axiom is equivalent to asserting that memory traces are never completely obliterated. The fruitfulness of the axiom depends on the fact that it frequently has face validity, that it usually can be supported, and that it is very hard to falsify. The latter would mean to demonstrate the complete obliteration of the traces of a given experience.

Note 1.5.4 The past is retained through its impact on the person (memory). What has happened earlier influences a person's present disposition and allows for predictions of the future. The concern of psychology is not with physically measured time, but with time as it exists *for* the person. The person's activities refer to the past, the present, and the future. The relations "before/after" and "simultaneous" are important, and subjective events are ordered according to them on an ordinal temporal scale. The basic terms for characterizing a person's activities temporally are as follows:

Primitive term 1.5.5 *When*

Primitive term 1.5.6 *After*

Primitive term 1.5.7 *Before*

Primitive term 1.5.8 *Now*

Note 1.5.9 In this book, time is always subjective (time for a person). The primitive temporal terms form a logical system. If A occurs *when* B occurs, then B occurs *when* A occurs. If A occurs *when* B occurs, and if B occurs *when* C occurs, then A occurs *when* C occurs. If A occurs *when* B occurs, and if B occurs *after* C occurs, then A occurs *after* C occurs. If A occurs *before* B occurs, and B occurs *before* C occurs, then A occurs *before* C occurs. And so on.

Definition 1.5.10 *"P remembers X"* = df *"P is aware of X having occurred before."*

Definition 1.5.11 *"P has forgotten X"* = df *"Before, P was aware of X occurring, but now, P is not aware of X having occurred before."*

Note 1.5.12 That P has forgotten X, in a given situation at a given time, does not imply anything definite about other situations and other times. Forgetting may be more or less context dependent.

Definition 1.5.13 *"P perceives X"* = df *"P is aware of X being present now."*

Definition 1.5.14 *"P expects X to occur"* = df *"P is aware that X is going to occur after now."*

Axiom 1.5.15 *P's awareness of the future consists of extrapolations from P's awareness of trends in the past.*

Note 1.5.16 Axiom 1.5.15 characterizes the process of learning in very general terms. "Extrapolation" means that a given trend is taken to continue. Given no other relevant information, an unchanging trend is expected to remain unchanged, increasing or decreasing trends are expected to continue, positively or negatively accelerated trends are expected to continue, and so on. Also previously established meanings are expected to be stable. This does not mean that one cannot anticipate unique and new events. If current trends continue, one may, for example, anticipate that they will reach critical values, lead to catastrophes, and so on. Such anticipations are based on combinations of previous information. However, basically, P's only guideline to the future is that it will be a continuation of the regularities of the past.

Corollary 1.5.17 *Learning to predict future events does not occur on the basis of trends in what "actually" happens, but on the basis of what P is aware of.* Proof: This follows directly from Axiom 1.5.15.

Note 1.5.18 Corollary 1.5.17 means that the lessons of experience are often hard to grasp. There may be highly regular objective patterns in what happens to or around a person, yet nothing is learned if the person does not recognize them. On the other hand, the fast and exceedingly complex socialization of children into a culture can take place only because they are provided with "precooked" experiences, that is, experiences prepared in easily recognizable and therefore, learnable forms.

Note 1.5.19 Although irreversibility is a fairly general characteristic of mental changes, and reflects a person's openness to experience, this is not the whole story. There are also processes that are *reversible* and, hence, closed to the influence of experience.

The hallmark of reversibility is the presence of *invariants* indicating that changes are only apparent or superficial, and can be completely and exactly undone. Among the most studied of these are the various principles of *conservation*, and the corresponding groups of reversible operations. Common to these is that they involve variations that do not, and cannot, make an irreversible difference. If a person believes that there are equal numbers of tokens in two piles, then no rearrangement of the tokens within each pile changes this belief. One rearrangement does not form context for judging the next one, precisely because each individual change is seen as completely reversible. The person believes that if two amounts are equal and nothing is added to or taken away from any one of them, then they must, necessarily, remain equal, in spite of changing appearances.

Note 1.5.20 The topic of reversible processes is widely ignored in psychology, outside the Piagetean tradition (Smith, 1993). Reversible processes occur in two different domains. First, they occur in closed systems of interpreting the world, where everything is effortlessly assimilated, and, hence, no contradictions and no learning can occur. Examples of this are basic trust or basic mistrust, ideas of persecution, religious and political convictions, and so on.

Second, reversible processes occur in all calculi and all uses of logic, such as derivations, proofs, analyses of possibilities, impossibilities and necessities. The use of logic presupposes that premises and meanings remain unchanged over time and shifting contexts.

Note 1.5.21 The reversible aspects of a person's processes pose a peculiar problem since they are not sensitive to experience. Nothing can shake the idea of conservation, once it is established. Similar closed systems are also frequently encountered in clinical work.

In conclusion: Persons are natural entities. Since both the psychologists and the individuals they try to study or help are persons, research and practice in psychology always involves *personal* encounters. Personal processes are characterized in terms of the five conceptual schemes of *subjectivity, intentionality, normativity, reflectivity* and *reversibility*.

Chapter 2

Acting

    Note 2.0.0 It is taken for granted here that a person is *active* rather than *passive*. By this is meant that personal activity is initiated and sustained from within, and never, as in the case of a puppet, wholly from without. This is consistent with the following axiom:

    Axiom 2.0.1 *A conscious person is continuously acting.*

    Note 2.0.2. The unceasing personal activities have been characterized in terms of the five broad categories described in chapter 1. Is it necessary, for the purpose of developing a psychologic, to further distinguish between different sorts of activities? An obvious and widely used distinction is between cognition and action. I argue that, for the purpose of formulating a psychologic, this distinction may not be important.

2.1. Cognizing and Doing

    Note 2.1.0 In ordinary language, many of the verbs descriptive of personal activities can be subsumed under two broad categories. One contains terms such as looking, listening, reading, and may be labeled *cognizing*. A second contains terms such as expressing, talking, writing, and may be labeled *doing*. The two categories can be distinguished by the type of goals involved. In cognizing, the goal is to achieve information about the situation, and in doing, the goal is to achieve a change in the situation. The two kinds of processes can be seen merged into one in the case of a blind or blindfolded person who is asked to identify an object. The hand movements are at the same time doing (turning the object around and hence, changing the situation) and cognizing (touching the object on all sides and hence, construing a coherent image of the object). In this case, doing is subordinated to a cognitive goal, but frequently the reverse situation occurs, that is, cognizing is subordinated to some action goal. In general, cognizing and doing are constantly coordinated.

    Note 2.1.1 It is generally recognized that the outcome of cognizing is subjective and that the structure of doing is intentional. However, it is equally true that the structure of cognizing is intentional and that the outcome of doing is subjective. Cognizing not only involves active components such as adjusting and directing ones sense organs (looking, listening, sniffing, touching), attending selectively to parts of the stimulus field, and so on, but also involves relying vicariously on available cues according to their estimated relevance for the projects at hand. Finally, attempts to understand involve trying out successive interpretations, and modifying them according to the outcome. Hence, cognizing is intentionally structured at all levels.

Similarly, doing and its outcomes are subjective. Even when it involves observable bodily movement and objectively measurable muscle contractions, these do not define *what* a person is doing or the *meaning* of the movements. Even when the doing has a well defined social meaning it may, for example, involve dissimulation on the part of the actor and hence, have a hidden subjective meaning. Finally, doing may occur without any objectively measurable concomitants. This is the case, for example, when a person intentionally refrains from saying something to another person and thereby conveys a message. What is done consists of intentionally *not* mentioning something which could have been mentioned. Another person who intentionally cognizes (interprets) this, becomes aware that something was *not* said that might have been said, and that this means something definite. In this case there may be efficient communication, even though nothing happens which could be objectively registered.

Note 2.1.2 In summary, a person's processes may be subdivided into cognizing and doing, according to what kind of goal is involved, but these are always intimately coordinated and are always both subjective and intentional. Almost all activities involve components of both cognizing and doing. One tries to see something clearly and one tries to perform a task. One can or cannot see clearly what one tries to see, and one can or cannot do what one tries to do. However, one cannot see something without opening one's eyes and directing them in a coordinated manner, accommodating the lens properly, and so on. Conversely, one cannot perform a difficult task, such as jumping over an obstacle without locating and evaluating it visually, without sensing the starting position of one's legs and one's body, and so on. Almost every meaningful subdivision of psychological activities leads to units which have numerous components of both cognizing and doing. In what follows, the two aspects are not differentiated. I use the term *act* to cover both "cognize" and "do." The reader is reminded that this usage of the term *act* departs from ordinary language where, for example, looking at something, listening to something, or interpreting something, are usually not referred to as acts.

Note 2.1.3 The notion of *acting*, as used here, refers to intentionally bringing about changes in a person's subjective world. The change brought about by an act is not an objective external outcome, but the outcome as it exists for the person. Objective results of an act which are not recognized by the actor have no psychological existence. Similarly, the acting itself is, for example, not an objectively measurable movement, but the movement or absence of movement as it exists for the person.

Note 2.1.4 In everyday life as well as in traditional scientific psychology there is a tendency to alternate between viewing psychological phenomena from within and from without. This is reflected in the use of terms such as "error," "bias," and "irrational," which all involve a characterization in terms of objective or external criteria. Contrary to this, psychology is here seen as involving the subjective only. As a consequence, error, bias, and irrationality enter only as they exist *for* someone. They involve recognition that one has made a mistake or has been misled in some way. This is a post hoc judgment that what one *now* recognizes as proper premises and implications differs from what one *then* assumed. I take it for granted that no one is subjectively irrational at any given moment, and that action is always a logical consequence of the momentary premises of the actor (Smedslund, 1990b, 1997b).

2.2 The Conditions of Acting

Note 2.2.0 Whether or not a person performs an act depends on whether or not the person *can* perform it, and on whether or not the person *tries to* perform it. In what follows, the central terms to be used, namely *can* and *try*, are left undefined, and are intended to retain their ordinary language meanings. Hence, "P can do A" means the same as "it is possible for P to do A", and "P tries to do A" means the same as "P attempts to do A" and "P makes an effort to do A."

Primitive term 2.2.1 *Can*

Primitive term 2.2.2 *Try*

Axiom 2.2.3 *P does A, if, and only if, P can do A and P tries to do A.*

Corollary 2.2.4 *If P does A, then P can do A, and P tries to do A.*
Proof: This follows directly from Axiom 2.2.3.

Corollary 2.2.5 *If P does not do A, then P cannot do A, or P does not try to do A, or P neither can nor tries to do A.*   Proof: This follows directly from Axiom 2.2.3.

Corollary 2.2.6 *If P can do A and P does not do A, then P does not try to do A.*   Proof: This follows directly from Axiom 2.2.3.

Corollary 2.2.7 *If P tries to do A and P does not do A, then P cannot do A.*
Proof: This follows directly from Axiom 2.2.3.

Note 2.2.8 Axiom 2.2.3 and its corollaries are very frequently used in everyday life. The conclusions about can and try also frequently form the basis for generalizations about a person's abilities, beliefs and wants in other contexts and at other times.

Note 2.2.9 The reader is reminded that these propositions apply equally well to what was labeled "cognizing" as to what was labeled "doing." Insert for "A" in propositions 2.2.3 to 2.2.7 above, for example, the cognitive task of discriminating between the tastes of Coca Cola and Pepsi Cola, and the doing task of building a house of playing cards.

2.3 The Conditions of Can

Primitive term 2.3.0 *Ability*

Primitive term 2.3.1 *Difficulty*

Note 2.3.2 Ability is a person variable and difficulty is a task variable. If the task is to jump over a hurdle, P's ability to jump is a person variable and the height of the hurdle is a task variable. It should be clear that these factors can be varied independently of each other. In what follows P and O are persons and A and B are tasks.

Axiom 2.3.3 *P can do A, if, and only if, P's ability to do A is greater than the difficulty of A.*

Theorem 2.3.4 *If P can and O cannot do A, then P has greater ability than O to do A.*   Proof: According to Axiom 2.3.3, P can do A, if, and only if, P's ability to do A is greater than the difficulty of doing A. It follows that, because P can do A, P's ability is greater than the difficulty of doing A. Also, according to Axiom 2.3.3, since O cannot do A, O's ability to do A is less than the difficulty of doing A. But, if P's ability is greater than and O's ability is less than the difficulty of A, then P's ability is greater than O's ability to do A. This proves the theorem.

Axiom 2.3.5 *The degree of exertion of P in doing A is inversely proportional to the size of the positive difference between the ability of P to do A and the difficulty of doing A.*

Note 2.3.6 A positive difference exists as long as the ability is higher than the difficulty. When there is a negative difference, that is, when the ability is lower than the difficulty, P can no longer do A. As the positive difference becomes greater, the amount of necessary exertion declines.

Note 2.3.7 Possible *symptoms* of exertion include physical tension, facial and bodily expressions of effort, preoccupation, lowered tolerance of disturbance, slowed performance, heightened frequency of errors and corrections, and the person's own statements about how it feels or felt to do A. The latter symptom implies that the act is reflective.

Theorem 2.3.8 *If P can do A with less exertion than O can do A, then P has greater ability than O to do A.*   Proof: According to Axiom 2.3.5, the degree of exertion of P in doing A is inversely proportional to the size of the positive difference between the ability of P to do A and the difficulty of doing A. Because P does A with less exertion than O, it follows that there is a greater positive difference between the ability of P and the difficulty of A than between the ability of O and the difficulty of A. From this is follows that P has greater ability to do A than O. This proves the theorem.

Theorem 2.3.9 *If, when both P and O can do A, it takes less increment in the difficulty of A to make O fail, than it takes to make P fail, then P has greater ability than O to do A.*   Proof: According to Axiom 2.3.3, P can do A, if, and only if, P's ability to do A is greater than the difficulty of doing A. It follows that failure occurs at the point where ability equals the difficulty. But, if it takes less increment in the difficulty of A to make O fail than it takes to make P fail, then P must have greater ability than O. This proves the theorem.

Theorem 2.3.10 *If, when both P and O cannot do A, it takes less decrement in the difficulty of A to make P able to do A than it takes to make O able to do A, then P has greater ability than O to do A.*   Proof: According to Axiom 2.3.3, P can do A, if, and only if, P's ability to do A is greater than the difficulty of doing A. But, if it takes less decrement in the difficulty of A to make P able to do A than it takes to make O able to do A, then P must have greater ability than O to do A. This proves the theorem.

Note 2.3.11 The preceding four theorems indicate four ways of determining the relative strength of two persons' abilities to do solve the same task. Conventional concepts of ability are generalized over categories of tasks, and are measured by probability of success rather than on simple pass and fail. These conventional concepts are not inconsistent with the elementary theorems presented here, but on the contrary, may be derived from them.

Theorem 2.3.12 *If P cannot do A and P can do B, then A is more difficult than B.*   Proof: According to Axiom 2.3.3,

P can do A, if, and only if, P's ability to do A is greater than the difficulty of doing A. From this it follows that the difficulty of A is higher than P's ability and the difficulty of B is lower than P's ability and hence, A is more difficult than B. This proves the theorem.

Theorem 2.3.13 *If P does A with more exertion than P does B, then A is more difficult than B.*   Proof: According to Axiom 2.3.5, the degree of exertion of P in doing A is inversely proportional to the size of the positive difference between the ability of P to do A and the difficulty of doing A. It follows that the size of the positive difference between P's ability and the difficulty of the task is smaller in the case of A than in the case of B. If P's ability is taken to be the same in the two cases, it follows that A is more difficult than B. This proves the theorem.

Theorem 2.3.14 *If, when P can do both A and B, it takes less decrement in P's ability to make P fail on A than it takes to make P fail on B, then A is more difficult than B.* Proof: According to Axiom 2.3.3, P can do A, if, and only if, P's ability to do A is greater than the difficulty of doing A. From this it follows that the difference between the difficulty of A and P's ability is less than the difference between the difficulty of B and P's ability and hence, A is more difficult than B. This proves the theorem.

Theorem 2.3.15 *If, when P cannot do A and P cannot do B, it takes more increment in P's ability to make P succeed doing A than it takes to make P succeed doing B, then A is more difficult than B.* Proof: It follows from Axiom 2.3.3, that when P cannot do A and P cannot do B, P's ability is less than the difficulty of doing A and doing B. From this it follows that if it takes more increment in P's ability to make him or her succeed in doing A than it takes to make him or her succeed in doing B, then A must be more difficult than B. This proves the theorem.

Note 2.3.16 The preceding four theorems indicate four ways of determining the relative difficulty of tasks for a person. Conventional measures of difficulty are generalized over many persons and measure difficulty in terms of probability of passing. However, these conventional measures do not contradict the fundamental measures of difficulty presented above but, on the contrary, may be derived from them.

Note 2.3.17 Theorems 2.3.4, 2.3.8, 2.3.9, and 2.3.10, comparing the abilities of two persons, all presuppose that the same task is equally difficult for the two. One can compare abilities only when difficulty is assumed to be constant. Similarly, theorems 2.3.12, 2.3.13, 2.3.14, and 2.3.15 comparing the difficulties of two tasks, all presuppose that the person's ability remains the same. One can compare difficulties only when ability is assumed to be constant.

Note 2.3.18 The relative difficulties of tasks may or may not be ordered in the same way for different persons, and the relative abilities of persons may or may not be ordered in the same way for different tasks. Also, the order found at one time may or may not be maintained at a later time. The study of ability of persons and difficulty of tasks is an empirical undertaking. Psychologic indicates the inferences that can be made under given conditions.

The following corollaries may be formulated concerning the relations among difficulty, ability, and exertion:

Corollary 2.3.19 *If P must exert him- or herself very much to do A, then P's ability to do A is only a little higher than the difficulty of A.* Proof: This follows directly from Axiom 2.3.5.

Corollary 2.3.20 *If P must exert him- or herself very little to perform A, then P's ability to perform A is much higher than the difficulty of A.* Proof: This follows directly from Axiom 2.3.5.

Corollary 2.3.21 *If P does A only with great exertion, and if P has much higher ability to do A than O, then it is very likely that O cannot do A.* Proof: This follows directly from Axiom 2.3.5.

Corollary 2.3.22 *If P performs A with little exertion and if P has lower ability than O, then O must do A with even less exertion.* Proof: This follows directly from Axiom 2.3.5.

Note 2.3.23 The preceding summarizes some of the conditions of can. The given propositions are continuously used in everyday life.

2.4 The Conditions of Trying

Note 2.4.0 *Try* is a primitive concept (2.2.2) and is another of the necessary conditions of acting (Axiom 2.2.3). In order to formulate the conditions of trying, some other concepts must be introduced.

Primitive term 2.4.1 *Good*

Primitive term 2.4.2 *Bad*

Primitive term 2.4.3 *Feel*

Definition 2.4.4 *"Value of X for P"* = df *"The degree to which X feels good versus bad to P."*

Note 2.4.5 The concept of *value* refers to position on the good/bad feeling dimension. Positive value is what feels good and negative value is what feels bad. Neutral value feels neither good nor bad.

Primitive term 2.4.6 *Exertion*

Note 2.4.7 The exertion involved in performing an act always enters as a factor in determining what a person will try to do. The term is not defined in the present system. It refers to the effort necessary to execute a given act. The effects of exertion on trying may be derived from the following axiom:

Axiom 2.4.8 *P wants to minimize exertion.*

Note 2.4.9 This axiom does not state that people are lazy, but only that a want to minimize exertion exists, among other wants. The extent to which it determines trying depends on the relative strengths of the entire set of wants and beliefs involved.

Corollary 2.4.10 *Given two alternatives for acting differing only in the estimated amount of exertion involved, P will choose the one P believes involves the least amount of exertion.* Proof: This follows directly from Axiom 2.4.8.

Definition 2.4.11 *"The expected utility of doing A, for P"* = df *"the product of the expected outcome value of A, for P, and the expected likelihood, for P, of A leading to that outcome."*

Axiom 2.4.12 *P tries to maximize expected utility.*

Corollary 2.4.13 *P tries to do A, if, and only if, A is the act which, for P, has the highest expected utility.* Proof: This follows directly from Axiom 2.4.12.

Note 2.4.14 Six propositions about trying derivable from Corollary 2.4.13 were included in my formalization of Bandura's theory of self-efficacy (Smedslund, 1978a, 1982c). These were designated as Theorems 1, 2, 3, 7, 8, and 9 in the original articles. In what follows, they are presented in a somewhat revised form and proved in the same order. The original theorem numbers are given in parentheses.

Corollary 2.4.15 (1) *If P wants to do A, and if P believes that P can do A, and if no other wants and beliefs intervene, then P will try to do A.* Proof: Because no other wants and beliefs intervene, doing A has the highest expected utility for P. Hence, it follows from Corollary 2.4.12 that P will try to do A.

Note 2.4.16 It is apparent from Corollary 2.4.13 that if no other wants and beliefs intervene, it is sufficient that the person wants to do A and believes that he or she can do A, for the person to try to do A. No specification of strength of want and belief is necessary. If, on the other hand, other wants and beliefs intervene, it is necessary that the product of the strength of the given want and the given belief exceed any product of any combination of these other wants and beliefs.

Corollary 2.4.17 (2) *If P wants to do A, and if P believes with complete certainty that P cannot do A, and no other wants and beliefs intervene, then P will not try to do A.* Proof: Because P is certain that P cannot do A, it follows that the corresponding belief-strength is zero. But if the belief-strength is zero, then the expected utility of trying to do A is zero, and, therefore, it follows from Corollary 2.4.13 that P will not try to do A.

Corollary 2.4.18 (3) *If P wants to do A, and if no other wants and beliefs intervene, then the stronger P's belief that P can do A, the more likely it is that P will try to do A.* Proof: Given a constant want to do A, and assuming that no other wants and beliefs intervene, it follows from Definition 2.4.11 that the expected utility is directly proportional to the strength of belief. Hence, assuming that the likelihood of trying a given act is directly proportional to the expected utility of the act, the corollary follows.

Corollary 2.4.19 (7) *If P believes that doing A is rightly required in situation S, and if P believes with certainty that P cannot do A in S, then, if no other wants and beliefs intervene, P will try to avoid S.* Proof: According to Axiom 1.3.9, a person wants to do what is right. But, P believes with certainty that P cannot do what is right in S. Therefore, because no other wants and beliefs intervene, P will try to avoid doing something wrong, namely to fail to do what is rightly required in S. Hence, P will try to avoid S. This proves the corollary.

Corollary 2.4.20 (8) *If P believes that doing A is rightly required in situation S, and if P believes with certainty that P can do A in S, then, if no other wants and beliefs intervene, P will not try to avoid S.* Proof: According to Axiom 1.3.9 a person wants to do what is right. Because P believes with certainty that P can do A, and, hence, can avoid doing something wrong, then, if no other wants and beliefs intervene, he or she has no reason to avoid S. Hence, the corollary is proved.

Corollary 2.4.21 (9) *If no other wants and beliefs intervene, the stronger P's belief that P can do A, the longer will P continue to try to do A in the face of repeated failure.* Proof: It follows from Axiom 3.5.1, that the strength of P's belief that P can do A is directly proportional to P's estimate of the likelihood that P can do A. Hence, the stronger P's belief that P can do A, the more likely P thinks it is that P can do A. Each repeated failure lowers P's estimate of the likelihood. It follows that the stronger the belief, the higher the initial likelihood, and the longer it takes to reduce the likelihood to zero, and consequently, the longer P will continue to try to do A. Hence, the corollary is proved.

Note 2.4.22 The preceding propositions rest on simplified assumptions. Even in the simplest choice situation of doing A versus not doing A, which is also an act, there are at least 10 determinants of trying involved, all logically independent of each other. First, there is the subjective likelihood that A leads to G. Second, there is the subjective likelihood that not-A leads to G. Furthermore, there is the subjective value of G given A, the subjective value of G, given not-A, the subjective value of not-G given A, and the subjective value of not-G given not-A. In addition to the preceding, there comes the subjective likelihood that P can do A, the subjective likelihood that P can refrain from doing A, and the exertion involved in doing A and in refraining from doing A. Although many of these can often be eliminated with some confidence, they re-enter the picture as possible factors when the results of a study indicate a deviation from the expected results. In other words, these variables are always there, although they frequently are assumed to be constant at 1.00 or 0.00. The list of 10 variables serves to call to attention the fact that a moral or other premium is often put on doing or refraining from doing something, regardless of the outcome. For example, it is sometimes better to have failed after trying, than to have failed without trying. Furthermore, persons may lack the necessary confidence to carry out an act or, as the case may be, to refrain from carrying it out. There may also be a positive premium on refraining from doing an act, regardless of outcome, and there may be a negative premium on trying and failing. Finally, nothing follows from the known subjective value of G about the subjective value of not-G, with or without having tried A.

Note 2.4.23 The deviations from the theoretical utility function observed in empirical research are generally open to reinterpretation. Frequently, many of the 10 variables mentioned are given only perfunctory attention. One seldom bothers to get estimates of all of the *subjective* magnitudes of likelihoods and values.

Note 2.4.24 A series of derivations from Axiom 2.4.12 are widely relied on in everyday life.

Corollary 2.4.25 *If P's strongest want is to achieve G, if P believes that trying to do A is the alternative with the highest likelihood of leading to G, and if P believes that P can perform A, then P will try to do A.* Proof: Because A is the act with the highest expected utility for P, the corollary follows directly from Axiom 2.4.12.

Corollary 2.4.26 *Given a number of action possibilities which P believes involve the same degree of exertion and have equiprobable outcomes, and that P believes that A leads to the outcome with the highest value, then P will try to do A.* Proof: Because the action possibilities have equiprobable outcomes and involve equal exertion, and because the outcome of A has the highest expected value, it follows that A has the highest expected utility for P, and hence, the corollary follows directly from Axiom 2.4.12.

Corollary 2.4.27 *If P's only want is to achieve G, if P believes that A and all alternative acts lead to G, if P believes that all the alternative acts involve the same amount of exertion as A, and if P tries to do A, then P believes that trying to do A is the alternative with the highest likelihood of leading to G.* Proof: According to Axiom 2.4.12, P tries to maximize expected utility and, according to Definition 2.4.11, expected utility is the product of expected value and the likelihood of achieving that value. Because the expected value of the alternative outcomes is a constant (= G), it follows that, because P prefers A, P must believe that A has the highest likelihood of leading to G. This proves the proposition.

Note 2.4.28 Although the preceding theorem is formally correct, it should be added that, in a case where the alternatives have equal expected utilities, a person may be forced to make a random choice. However, random choice situations are rare in everyday life and Corollary 2.4.27 is usually helpful.

Corollary 2.4.29 *If P believes that there are a number of possible actions with equiprobable outcomes and involving equal exertion, and if P tries to do A, then A is the alternative from which P expects the highest outcome value.*   Proof: Because P tries to do A, it follows from Axiom 2.4.12 that P believes that A is the act with the highest expected utility. But, P also believes that the alternatives involve equal exertion and have equiprobable outcomes. Therefore, P must also believe that A is the alternative with the highest outcome value.

Note 2.4.30 The same comment applies here as in the case of Corollary 2.4.27. In the case of several alternatives with equal expected utilities the person may be forced to select one at random. Again, such cases are rare and do not detract from the usefulness of corollary 2.4.29.

Note 2.4.31 Corollaries 2.4.27 and 2.4.29 are among the most frequently used formulae for estimating the relative strength of a person's beliefs and wants in everyday life.

Corollary 2.4.32 *If P does not believe that P can do A, then P does not try to do A.*   Proof: If P does not believe that he or she can do A, it follows that P does not believe that trying to do A will lead to the wanted outcome. This means that the subjective likelihood of achieving the outcome is zero. But, if the likelihood of achieving the outcome is zero, then according to Definition 2.4.11, the expected utility of trying to do A is also zero. From this and from Corollary 2.4.13, it follows that P will not try to do A and hence, the corollary is proved.

Note 2.4.33 In summary, it has been argued that cognizing and overt action have the same subjectivity and intentionality and can be treated together from the point of view of psychologic. Hence, the formulae relating to acting cover both cognizing and overt action. An act is executed only when the person both can do it and tries to do it. A person can do an act only when the person's ability is higher than the difficulty of the act. A person tries to do an act if, and only if, for this person, the act has the highest expected utility. The three factors involved are likelihood that trying to do something will lead to the goal, the exertion believed to be involved, and the subjective value of that goal. The likelihood that trying something will lead to a goal is composed of the likelihood that one will succeed in doing the act and the likelihood that the act leads to the expected goal.

Chapter 3

Wanting and Believing

Note 3.0.0 Two main constituents of personal activities are *wanting* and *believing*. These two terms are basic, but undefined in the present system.

3.1 *Wanting*

Primitive term 3.1.1 *Want*

Note 3.1.2 At any moment in time a person is aware of alternatives, and chooses one before the others. This ubiquitous phenomenon of preference is the basis for the concept of *want*.

Axiom 3.1.3 *P wants X, if, and only if, other things equal, P prefers X to not-X.*

Note 3.1.4 Because anything may be inserted for "X," this axiom refers to every conceivable type of want, including both wants to achieve and to maintain positive goals, and wants to avoid or to escape negative goals. In all cases, wanting involves a direction toward something. It is a central concept in the intentional scheme described in chapter 1.

Theorem 3.1.3 *A conscious person is continuously wanting something.*
Proof: According to Axiom 2.0.1, a conscious person is continuously active. Because, according to Axiom 1.2.4, acting is intentional, that is, by Definition 1.2.3, directed by preference, and because, according to Axiom 3.1.1, to be directed by preference implies wanting, the theorem follows.

Note 3.1.4 What persons want cannot be exhaustively categorized. It may range from getting rid of a minor itch to world peace. There is, in principle, no limit to what a person could want. However, there are things that all persons *must* want, because they are persons. Some of these wants are treated in chapters 5 and 6. Finally, what is wanted is linked with the concepts of *good* (2.4.1), *bad* (2.4.2), and *feel* (2.4.3). Persons want to feel good and want to avoid feeling bad (see the following).

Note 3.1.5 The distinction between reflective and unreflective awareness (Definitions 1.4.1 and 1.4.2) also applies to wanting, which is a basic aspect of awareness. Because it is P who wants, P cannot be unaware of the want. However, P may be either reflectively or unreflectively aware of the want, and hence, may or may not be able to talk about it.

Definition 3.1.6 *"P reflectively wants X"* = df *"P is aware THAT P wants X."*

Corollary 3.1.7 *If P reflectively wants X, then P can talk about wanting X.* Proof: This follows directly from Axiom 1.4.11, which states that P can talk about what P is reflectively aware of, and only that.

Corollary 3.1.8 *If P can talk about P's want of X, then P is reflectively aware of that want.* Proof: This follows directly from Axiom 1.4.11.

Definition 3.1.9 *"P unreflectively wants X"* = df *"P is not aware THAT P wants X."*

Corollary 3.1.10 *If P unreflectively wants X, then P cannot talk about that want.* Proof: This follows directly from Axiom 1.4.11.

Corollary 3.1.11 *If P cannot talk about P's want of X, then P's want of X is unreflective.* Proof: This follows directly from Axiom 1.4.11.

Note 3.1.12 The conjunction of corollaries 3.1.7, 3.1.8, 3.1.10, and 3.1.11 is equivalent to Axiom 1.4.11 as it applies to the awareness of wants.

3.2 Good and Bad

Note 3.2.0 The primitive terms *good* (2.4.1), *bad* (2.4.2), and *feel* (2.4.3) have already been introduced, as well as the concept of *value* (2.4.4). The "value of X for P" is defined as "the degree to which X feels good versus bad to P." Positive value is what feels good and negative value is what feels bad.

Axiom 3.2.1 *P wants to feel good and wants to avoid feeling bad.*

Note 3.2.2 There are, in principle, no limits to what can have positive and negative value for a person. This also means that there are no limits to what a person can want.

Note 3.2.3 Wanting to feel good and to avoid feeling bad are often seen as involving selfish pursuits. However, as used here, these terms apply equally well to altruistic concerns. Even when a person sacrifices his or her life to save someone else, it is a choice of the alternative expected to yield the highest available positive and/or the lowest available negative value.

Corollary 3.2.4 *If P wants X, then P believes attainment of X will yield an increment in positive or a decrement in negative value.* Proof: This follows directly from Axiom 3.2.1.

Corollary 3.2.5 *If P wants to avoid X, then P believes that attainment of X will make P feel bad.* Proof: This follows directly from Axiom 3.2.1.

Corollary 3.2.6 *If P wants X rather than Y, then P believes that attaining X will make P feel better than attaining Y.* Proof: This follows directly from Axiom 3.2.1.

Corollary 3.2.7 *If P believes that attaining X will make P feel better than attaining Y, then P wants X more than P wants Y.* Proof: This follows directly from Axiom 3.2.1.

Note 3.2.8 It is necessary to make a distinction between attainment of a goal and the fulfillment of a want. It is possible to attain a goal and be disappointed and also to be overwhelmed. The fulfillment of a want may be characterized as follows:

Axiom 3.2.9 *A want is fulfilled if, and only if, and to the extent that, the expected increment in positive or decrement in negative value occurs.*

Axiom 3.2.10 *A want is frustrated if, and only if, and to the extent that, the expected increment in positive or decrement in negative value does not occur.*

Note 3.2.11 It is obviously possible for P to experience value, that is, feel good or bad, without any already existing wants. Examples of this are an unexpected gift or an unexpected bill.

Note 3.2.12 A combination of several values with the same sign (positive or negative) yields a stronger resultant value. Also, a combination of values with different signs subtract from each other. This can be expressed in the following axiom:

Axiom 3.2.13 *If two positive or two negative values, p1 and p2, occur at the same time, they combine in such a way that p1 & p2 > p1, and p1 & p2 > p2. If a positive (p1) and a negative (p2) value occur at the same time, they combine in such a way that p1 & p2 < p1, and p1 & p2 > p2.*

Note 3.2.14 Here, as throughout this work, the quantification of variables is very weak. More refined statements can only be arrived at through empirical work in specific contexts, but then, the results probably will be of little general interest.

Note 3.2.15 *Why* does P anticipate feeling good or bad upon achievement of X? One type of answer is historical. According to Axiom 1.5.15, a person's awareness of the future consists of extrapolations from that person's awareness of trends in the past. Hence, if X has yielded good or bad outcomes in the past, then the person expects it to continue to yield the same outcomes in the future. Generalizing beyond simple repetitions of an identical situation X, the following theorem also applies:

Theorem 3.2.16 *If, for P, there is a certain positive or negative value in X1, then P will expect the same positive or negative value in X2 to the extent that P is aware of what P takes to be relevant similarities between X1 and X2*   Proof: According to Axiom 1.5.15, P's awareness of the future consists of extrapolations from P's awareness of trends in the past. Hence, P will expect equally valued outcomes to the extent that P regards X1 and X2 as similar in relevant ways. This proves the theorem.

Note 3.2.17 The question of what leads to positively and negatively valued outcomes, yields only a circular answer, namely, that it depends on what the person wants, which again depends on what yields positive and negative value, and so on. At the level of psychological analysis, the question of what in fact, evokes feeling good and bad and hence, want, can only be answered by studying actual persons in actual situations.

Note 3.2.18 Another type of answer to the question of what leads to feeling good and bad involves the concept of need. Need differs from want in that it is not linked to beliefs about definite means and definite goals. A need to express him or herself artistically may exist in a person and merely be manifested in general dissatisfaction and unrest. Given paper and crayons, the person may start to experience strong pleasure and, from then on, the person may want to draw. In connection with this, the general dissatisfaction and unrest may diminish. A need is directedness without a goal.

Finally, feeling good and feeling bad may be explained at the level of neural processes, but this lies outside psychology proper.

Note 3.2.19 Pleasure and pain are located on a single dimension, separated by an indifference point. A person will always prefer what is relatively more pleasurable and less painful to what is relatively less pleasurable and more painful.

Note 3.2.20 The concept of *want* is linked to preference by Axiom 3.1.3, but not yet to action. In order to do this, one needs to link wanting and trying by means of the following proposition:

Theorem 3.2.21 *If P wants A, then, if no other factors intervene, P tries to achieve A.*   Proof: According to Axiom 3.1.3, if P wants A, then P prefers A to not-A. But, because, according to Axiom 2.0.1, a person is continuously active, and because no other factors intervene, P must choose between trying to achieve A and not trying to achieve A. Because P prefers A to not-A, it follows that trying to achieve A has the highest expected utility for P. Hence, according to Axiom 2.4.11, P must try to achieve A. By this the theorem is proved.

3.3 *Strength of Wants*

Primitive term 3.3.0 *Strength*

Note 3.3.1 There are, in principle, three ways of estimating the strength of a want. These correspond to conceptual links between strength and three other variables, namely expected increment in positive/decrement in negative value, dominance over competing wants, and direct reflective awareness.

Axiom 3.3.2 *The strength of P's want of X is directly proportional to the amount of increment in positive or decrement in negative value that P believes will occur when X is attained.*

Corollary 3.3.3 *If P's want of A is stronger than P's want of B, then P believes that the amount of increment in positive or decrement in negative value will be higher on attaining A than on attaining B.* Proof: This follows directly from Axiom 3.3.2.

Corollary 3.3.4 *If P believes that the amount of increment in positive or decrement in negative value will be higher on attaining A than on attaining B, then P's want of A is stronger than P's want of B.* Proof: This follows directly from Axiom 3.3.2.

Axiom 3.3.5 *P's want A is stronger than P's want B, if, and only if, when A and B are in conflict, and no other factors intervene, P tries to act according to A and not according to B.*

Definition 3.3.6 *"For P, two wants are in conflict"* = df *"For P, acting according to one of the two wants is incompatible with acting according to the other."*

Note 3.3.7 What, for P, is acting according to a given want, cannot be determined from knowledge of that want alone. One must also know P's relevant beliefs. If P wants to visit a certain cinema and also wants to visit a certain restaurant, one cannot decide on the basis of this alone, which want P is acting in accordance with, when taking a given bus. In order to make this decision one has to know where P believes the cinema and the restaurant are situated, and where P believes the bus is going. From the preceding it also follows that one cannot decide from knowing P's two wants, whether they are in conflict or not. This only becomes clear when one, for example, comes to know that P believes that the cinema and the restaurant are situated so far apart that a visit to one of them precludes a visit to the other one, given the available time.

Note 3.3.8 The following two corollaries are very frequently used in everyday life:

Corollary 3.3.9 *If P's want A is stronger than P's want B, then, when the wants are in conflict and no other factors intervene, P will try to act according to A and not according to B.* Proof: This follows directly from Axiom 3.3.5.

Corollary 3.3.10 *If P tries to act according to want A and not according to want B, when the wants are in conflict and no other factors intervene, then P's want A is stronger than P's want B.* Proof: This follows directly from Axiom 3.3.5.

Note 3.3.11 The expression "other factors" in Axiom 3.3.5 and in Corollaries 3.3.9 and 3.3.10 refers to other wants, beliefs, and relevant abilities (can).

Corollary 3.3.12 *If P's want A is stronger than P's want B, and the wants are in conflict, and if X can be perceived either as Y or not-Y, or as Z or not-Z, and if Y or not-Y is taken by P to be relevant for the project of achieving the goal of want A, and Z or not-Z is taken by P to be relevant for the project of achieving the goal of want B, then P will perceive X as Y or not-Y, and not as Z or not-Z.* Proof: According to Axiom 3.3.5, since P's want A is stronger than P's want B, P will act according to want A and not according to want B. But, according to Theorem 1.2.10, if P acts in order to achieve the goal of want A, then P will take into account what he or she takes to be relevant for the project of achieving that goal. Because Y or not-Y is taken by P to be relevant for the project of achieving the goal of want A, it follows that P will take into account, that is, perceive X as Y or not-Y, and not as Z or not-Z.

Note 3.3.13 In everyday life Corollary 3.3.12 is frequently applied in predicting how people will be perceptually selective according to their momentary dominant wants.

Note 3.3.14 If two wants are *not* in conflict, their strengths may combine. In order to formulate the conditions for such a combination, a definition of *compatibility* is needed:

Definition 3.3.15 *"Two wants are compatible"* = df *"Acting according to one of the two wants can be combined with acting according to the other."*

Note 3.3.16 Two wants may be in conflict with respect to some ways of acting and compatible with respect to some other ways of acting. The latter are taken to lead towards both goals at the same time.

Theorem 3.3.17 *If the wants W1 and W2, are compatible, then they combine in such a way that W1 & W2 > W1 and W1 & W2 > W2.* Proof: According to Axiom 3.3.2, the strength of a want is directly proportional to the expected increment in value. Because, according to Axiom 3.2.13, values combine in such a way that the combination is stronger than each of the components, it follows that wants combine in the same way. Hence, the theorem follows.

Corollary 3.3.18 *P's description of the strength of P's want A is correct if, and only if, P regards it as correct.*   Proof: This follows directly from Axiom 1.4.32.

Note 3.3.19 P's estimate of the strength of P's wants has face validity. You are the sole judge of your own reflective experience. The preceding means that, as already anticipated, there are altogether, three ways of estimating the strength of wants, namely relying on expectancy of value (Axiom 3.3.2), dominance (Axiom 3.3.5) and direct report (Corollary 3.3.18). From this the following six theorems may be derived:

Theorem 3.3.20 *If P believes that the amount of increment in positive or decrement in negative value will be greater upon attaining the goal of want A than upon attaining the goal of want B, then P will try to act according to want A and not according to want B, if A and B are in conflict, and no other factors intervene.*   Proof: If P believes that the amount of increment in positive or decrement in negative value will be greater on attaining the goal of A than on attaining the goal of B, then, according to Axiom 3.3.2, want A is stronger than want B. But, according to Axiom 3.3.5, if P's want A is stronger than P's want B, then, when the wants are in conflict and no other factors intervene, P will try to act according to A and not according to B. By this the theorem is proved.

Theorem 3.3.21 *If P tries to act according to want A and not according to want B, when these are in conflict and no other factors intervene, then P believes that the amount of increment in positive or decrement in negative value will be greater on attaining A than on attaining B.*   Proof: If P tries to act according to A and not according to B, when the wants are in conflict and no other factors intervene, then, according to Axiom 3.3.5, want A is stronger than want B. But, according to Axiom 3.3.1, if want A is stronger than want B, then P believes that the increment in positive or decrement in negative value will be greater on attaining the goal of A than on attaining the goal of B. Hence, the theorem is proved.

Theorem 3.3.22 *If P believes that the amount of increment in positive or decrement in negative value will be greater on attaining the goal of want A than on attaining the goal of want B, then P will describe want A as stronger than want B, given that A and B are in conflict, and that no other factors intervene.*   Proof: If P believes that the amount of increment in positive value or decrement in negative value will be greater on attaining the goal of want A than on attaining the goal of want B, then according to Axiom 3.3.2, want A is stronger than want B. But, according to Corollary 3.3.18, if want A is stronger than want B, then P will describe want A as stronger than want B. By this the theorem is proved.

Theorem 3.3.23 *If P describes want A as stronger than want B, then P believes that the amount of increment in positive or decrement in negative value will be greater on attaining the goal of want A than on attaining the goal of want B, given that A and B are in conflict, and that no other factors intervene.*   Proof: If P describes want A as stronger than want B, then, according to Corollary 3.3.18, want A is stronger than want B. But, if A is stronger than B, then according to Axiom 3.3.1, P believes that the amount of increment in positive or decrement in negative value will be greater on attaining the goal of A than on attaining the goal of B, given that A and B are in conflict, and that no other factors intervene. By this the theorem is proved.

Theorem 3.3.24 *If P tries to act according to want A and not according to want B, when these are in conflict and no other factors intervene, then P will describe want A as stronger than want B.*   Proof: If P tries to act according to want A and not according to want B, when these are in conflict and no other factors intervene, then according to Axiom 3.3.5, want A is stronger than want B. But, according to Corollary 3.3.18, if want A is stronger than want B, then P will describe want A as stronger than want B. This proves the theorem.

Theorem 3.3.25 *If P describes want A as stronger than want B, when these are in conflict, and no other factors intervene, then P will try to act according to want A and not according to want B.*   Proof: If P describes want A as stronger than want B when these are in conflict and no other factors intervene, then according to Corollary 3.3.18, want A is stronger than want B. But, according to Axiom 3.3.5, if want A is stronger than want B, then P will try to act according to want A and not according to want B. By this the theorem is proved.

3.4 Believing

Primitive term 3.4.0 Believe

Note 3.4.1 Believe is used here, instead of the closely related *think*. The concept of *belief* expresses what the person takes to be the case.

Axiom 3.4.2 *P believes X, if, and only if, for P, X is the case.*

Note 3.4.3 "For P, X is the case" should not be confused with "X exists for P," which is the definition of awareness. The latter refers to an unconditional relationship. If X is a phenomenon in P's awareness, then it cannot be wrong that P is aware of X. A belief, on the other hand, refers to *reality* and hence, may be correct or incorrect. Beliefs are usually wholly or partly based on other beliefs. The general formula is: P believes that X is the case because P believes that Y is the case because P believes that Z is the case because. . . . In other words, beliefs usually occur in mutually supporting systems.

Definition 3.4.4 *"X is the case"* = df *"X is consistent with everything else which is the case."*

Note 3.4.5 The preceding definition introduces one necessary and sufficient characteristic of what is the case, namely that it must be consistent with everything else that is the case. Hence, consistency is taken as the ultimate criterion of reality. What is inconsistent cannot represent a reality and cannot be acted on. If two beliefs are inconsistent, at least one of them must be false. If two beliefs are consistent, they may or may not be false.

Note 3.4.6 There is, in principle, no limit to what a person could believe. It is very difficult to imagine a belief that a person could not possibly hold, given a freedom to manipulate the circumstances.

Theorem 3.4.7 *A conscious person is continuously believing something.* Proof: According to Axiom 2.0.1 a conscious person is continuously acting. But, according to Corollary 2.4.12 acting always involves beliefs (about the expected utility). Hence, the theorem follows.

Note 3.4.8 Just as there are reflective and unreflective wants, there are reflective and unreflective beliefs.

Definition 3.4.9 *"P reflectively believes X "* = df *"P is aware THAT P believes X."*

Theorem 3.4.10 *If P reflectively believes X, then P can talk about that belief.*   Proof: This follows from Axiom 1.4.11.

Theorem 3.4.11 *If P can talk about P's belief X, then P reflectively believes X.*   Proof: This follows from Axiom 1.4.11.

Note 3.4.12 P may be reflectively aware of his or her belief X, and yet not talk about it. Only the *ability* to talk about it is involved here.

Definition 3.4.13 *"P unreflectively believes X"* = df *"P believes X, but is not aware THAT P believes this."*

Theorem 3.4.14 *If P unreflectively believes X, then P cannot talk about that belief.*   Proof: This follows from Axiom 1.4.11.

Theorem 3.4.15 *If P believes X, but cannot talk about this belief, then that belief is unreflective.*   Proof: This follows from Axiom 1.4.11.

Note 3.4.16 The conjunction of Theorems 3.4.10, 3.4.11, 3.4.14, and 3.4.15 corresponds to Axiom l.4.11 as it applies to the domain of beliefs.

Note 3.4.17 Because it is P who believes, P cannot be unaware of a belief, and cannot avoid taking it into account. However, P may be only unreflectively aware of the belief and hence, may be unable to talk about it.

Note 3.4.18 In the case of an individual with multiple personalities, P1 may be strictly unaware of a belief or want of P2, whereas within one person, there must be at least unreflective awareness of beliefs and wants. In the same way as reflective ones, unreflective beliefs and wants also guide a person's activities.

3.5 Strength of Beliefs

Note 3.5.0 As in the case of wants, there are three ways of estimating the strength of a belief. These correspond to conceptual links between strength and three other variables, namely likelihood of truth, dominance over competing beliefs, and reflective awareness.

Axiom 3.5.1 *The strength of P's belief X, is directly proportional to P's estimate of the likelihood that X is the case.*

Corollary 3.5.2 *If P's belief A is stronger than P's belief B, then P's estimate of the likelihood of A is higher than P's estimate of the likelihood of B.* Proof: This follows directly from Axiom 3.5.1.

Corollary 3.5.3 *If P's estimate of the likelihood of A is higher than P's estimate of the likelihood of B, then P's belief A is stronger than P's belief B.* Proof: This follows directly from Axiom 3.5.1.

Axiom 3.5.4 *P's belief A is stronger than P's belief B, if, and only if, when A and B are in conflict, and no other factors intervene, P tries to act according to A and not according to B.*

Definition 3.5.5 *"Two beliefs are in conflict"* = df *"Acting according to one of the beliefs is incompatible with acting according to the other one."*

Note 3.5.6 The direct proportionality to likelihood as well as the preference for acting in accordance with the stronger belief, when the beliefs are in conflict and no other factors intervene, are propositions that follow from what is *meant* by strength of a belief, but are not definitions.

Corollary 3.5.7 *P's description of the strength of P's belief A is correct if, and only if, P regards it as correct.* Proof: This follows directly from Axiom 1.4.32.

Note 3.5.8 The preceding means that there are, altogether, three ways of estimating the strength of beliefs, namely relying on likelihood (Axiom 3.5.1), dominance (Axiom 3.5.4), and direct report (Corollary 3.5.7). From these, six theorems may be derived.

Theorem 3.5.9 *If P believes that A is more likely to be true than B, then P tries to act according to belief A and not according to belief B, when the beliefs are in conflict and no other factors intervene.*   Proof: If P believes that A is more likely to be true than B, then, according to Axiom 3.5.1, P's belief A is stronger than P's belief B. But, according to Axiom 3.5.4, it then follows that P will try to act according to belief A and not according to belief B. Hence, the theorem is proved.

Theorem 3.5.10 *If P tries to act according to belief A and not according to belief B, when the beliefs are in conflict and no other factors intervene, then P believes that A is more likely to be true than B.*   Proof: If P tries to act according to belief A and not according to belief B, then, according to Axiom 3.5.4, P's belief A is stronger than P's belief B. But, according to Axiom 3.5.1, it then follows that P believes that A is more likely to be true than B. Hence, the theorem is proved.

Theorem 3.5.11 *If P believes that A is more likely to be true than B, then P will describe the belief A as stronger than the belief B.*   Proof: If P believes that A is more likely to be true than B, then, according to Axiom 3.5.1, P's belief A is stronger than P's belief that B. But, if P's belief that A is stronger than P's belief B, then according to Corollary 3.5.7, P will describe belief A as stronger than belief B. Hence, the theorem is proved.

Theorem 3.5.12 *If P describes belief A as stronger than belief B, then P believes that A is more likely to be true than B.*   Proof: If P describes belief A as stronger than belief B, then according to Corollary 3.5.7, P's belief A is stronger than P's belief B. But, if P's belief A is stronger than P's belief B, then according to Axiom 3.5.1, P believes that A is more likely to be true than B. Hence, the theorem is proved.

Theorem 3.5.13 *If P tries to act according to belief A and not according to belief B, when the beliefs are in conflict and no other factors intervene, then P will describe belief A as stronger than belief B.*   Proof: If P tries to act according to belief A and not according to belief B, when the beliefs are in conflict and no other factors intervene, then, according to Axiom 3.5.4, P's belief A is stronger than P's belief B. But, if P's belief A is stronger than P's belief B, then, according to Corollary 3.5.7, P will describe belief A as stronger than belief B. This proves the theorem.

Theorem 3.5.14 *If P describes belief A as stronger than belief B, then when the beliefs are in conflict and no other factors intervene, P will try to act according to belief A and not according to belief B.* Proof: If P describes belief A as stronger than belief B, when the beliefs are in conflict and no other factors intervene, then according to Corollary 3.5.7, belief A is stronger than belief B. But, if belief A is stronger than belief B, then, according to Axiom 3.5.4, P will try to act according to belief A and not according to belief B. This proves the theorem.

3.6 Parallels and Interplay Between Wants and Beliefs

Note 3.6.0 There is an obvious parallel between the conceptual structures surrounding wants and beliefs. Want is to fulfillment as belief is to confirmation. Goal attainment may or may not fulfill a want, and may or may not confirm a belief. Furthermore, awareness in both cases may be mistaken. The experience of fulfillment at having passed an exam may turn out to be premature if there was a printing error in the list of results. The belief that the exam was passed may also have been due to an erroneous perception of the list of results, which became evident by moving closer and adjusting the light.

Note 3.6.1 The analogy between wants and beliefs also extends in other directions. Feeling good is linked to the fulfillment of a want through Axiom 3.2.9. Feeling good may also be linked to the confirmation of a belief in the following way:

Axiom 3.6.2 *P wants to believe what is the case.*

Note 3.6.3 This axiom asserts that there is always a want to know the truth. It asserts nothing about the strength of this want, and it does not deny the possibility that other wants may occasionally be stronger. There obviously exist cases of denial of reality and cases of reluctance to know the truth.

Theorem 3.6.4 *The confirmation of a belief entails feeling good.*
Proof: The confirmation of a belief indicates that it corresponds to what is the case. Therefore, according to Axiom 3.6.2, confirmation is the fulfillment of a want. But, according to Axiom 3.2.9, fulfillment of a want involves feeling good and hence, the theorem follows.

Theorem 3.6.5 *The nonconfirmation of a belief entails feeling bad.*
Proof: The nonconfirmation of a belief indicates that it does not correspond to what is the case. Therefore, according to Axiom 3.6.2, nonconfirmation is the nonfulfillment of a want. But, according to Axiom 3.2.9, the nonfulfillment of a want entails feeling bad. Hence, the theorem follows.

Corollary 3.6.6 *The fulfillment of a want involves confirmation.*
Proof: According to Corollary 3.2.6, a want involves a belief that goal attainment entails feeling good. Therefore, feeling good when attaining a goal involves the confirmation of a belief.

Theorem 3.6.7 *P wants to resolve relevant ambiguity.* Proof: A relevantly ambiguous situation involves conflicting beliefs of undecided validity bearing on a project at hand. No confirmation occurs. But, according to Theorems 3.6.4 and 3.6.5, confirmation entails feeling good and nonconfirmation entails feeling bad. Therefore, the resolution of relevant ambiguity and hence, confirmation of some belief, is expected to lead to feeling good and, according to Axiom 3.2.1, is wanted.

Theorem 3.6.8 *P wants to resolve relevant ambivalence.* Proof: An ambivalent situation involves conflicting wants of approximately equal strength. Therefore P cannot act and hence, there is no fulfillment of wants. The resolution of ambivalence means that P can act and hence, achieve the fulfillment of wants and the corresponding good feeling. Because, according to Axiom 3.2.1, P wants to feel good and wants to avoid feeling bad, it follows that P wants to resolve relevant ambivalence.

Note 3.6.9 Theorems 3.6.7 and 3.6.8 concern the resolution of ambiguity and ambivalence relevant for a person's ongoing projects. They do not exclude the existence of vast areas of ambiguity and ambivalence in a person's subjective world, which are irrelevant to the person's dominant concerns and hence, have remained unresolved.

Note 3.6.10 The case of normative wants and beliefs has already been treated in section 1.3. It was shown that in this area there is a rigid connection between belief and want (Axiom 1.3.9: P wants to do what P believes is right, and wants not to do what P believes is wrong).

3.7 Wants and Beliefs About Existence

Note 3.7.0 It has already been pointed out (3.2.2, 3.4.6) that in principle, there are no limits to what persons can want and believe. Nevertheless, there are some wants and beliefs common to all persons. Among them are those having to do with the existence of individual selves, on the one hand, and of a shared world, on the other hand. Everyone believes that he or she exists, that others exist, and that there is a shared world out there.

Axiom 3.7.1 *P reflectively believes that P exists and that other persons exist.*

Note 3.7.2 Everyone takes him or herself unreflectively for granted. This is especially clear in anticipating outcomes of interactive situations in which oneself is involved and in which one's own impact influences events. However, persons also reflectively believe that they *exist* as an entity. The distinctions between "I" and "Me," "I" and "It," and "I" and "You" are part of ordinary language. The firm belief in one's own and the other one's existence as persons, and in a shared world, must be taken for granted.

Corollary 3.7.3 *Every person reflectively believes in the possibility of his or her nonexistence.* Proof: This follows from Axiom 3.7.1.

Note 3.7.4 The reflective awareness *that* one exists, means that there is awareness of the possibility of nonexistence, that is, death. The empirically based knowledge of mortality similarly entails immortality as a possibility, explored in myths and legends.

Axiom 3.7.5. *Every person reflectively wants to continue to exist.*

Note 3.7.6 Although the want to continue to exist is one of the strongest that persons have, it is sometimes weaker than the want to escape from the suffering of life. In line with the general distinction between unreflective and reflective acting one may, roughly, distinguish between spontaneous and premeditated suicide attempts. The spontaneous suicide attempt occurs when the person is overwhelmed by accumulated suffering and acts in a here-and-now context. The premeditated suicide attempt is planned over time and involves reflective awareness, in the context of the person's total life situation. Obviously, suicide attempts may involve intermediate or mixed states of awareness.

Corollary 3.7.7 *If a person attempts suicide, then that person has a want to die, which is stronger than the want to continue to live.* Proof: According to Axiom 3.7.5, every person wants to continue to exist. But, because the person tries to cease to exist, it follows from Axiom 3.3.5, that the want to cease to exist is stronger than the want to continue living. Hence, the corollary follows.

Note 3.7.8 People's existential problems are closely linked with religious concerns. Life is sacred, whereas the present concept of *strength of want* is profane. Hence, the slightly jarring tone of the proof of Corollary 3.7.7. It is also apparent that the possibilities of achieving eternal life and the conditions of this future life are almost always linked with *moral* considerations, that is, with the way in which the person acts relative to the norm-system of the given culture. Sinners are generally condemned to hell, or to impoverished conditions in future existences (reincarnation).

Note 3.7.9 There remains a set of beliefs common to all persons, namely that what they see as self-evident is also seen as such by everyone else, that everyone believes that everyone else believes that the beliefs in self-evidence are shared, and so on.

Note 3.7.10 Self-evidence has to do with the meaning of words making up a proposition. What is regarded as self-evidently true is what cannot be otherwise, given that words mean what they are taken to mean. For example, someone who is surprised must have experienced something unexpected. This is taken to be self-evident simply because of what the words mean. The consensus of beliefs about self-evidence can be studied in several ways. First, one can directly investigate the extent to which people regard a proposition as self-evidently true. Second, one may negate the proposition. To the extent that everyone judges the negation to be absurd and senseless, the status of the proposition as consensually self-evident is strengthened. Third, one may study whether the implications that people draw from the proposition are also judged to be self-evident. All axioms, corollaries and theorems in this book are intended to be consensually self-evident.

Note 3.7.11 The axiom to follow has to do with what persons take for granted about the shared nature of consensually self-evident psychological propositions. It is one of the most important principles of psychological common sense.

Axiom 3.7.12 *If everyone takes a psychological proposition X to be self-evident, then everyone believes that everyone else takes X to be self-evident, everyone believes that everyone else believes that everyone else takes X to be self-evident, everyone believes that everyone else believes that everyone else believes that everyone else takes X to be self-evident, and so on.*

Note 3.7.13 It follows from the preceding axiom that one may derive at least three other propositions from every consensually self-evident psychological proposition. This enhances the power and applicability of the system. In order to illustrate this, let X be equal to Theorem 5.1.14 which reads: *Every person wants to be treated with respect and wants to behave respectably.* Assuming that this theorem is consensually self-evident, we can derive the following three new theorems:

Theorem 5.1.14.a *Everyone believes that everyone wants to be treated with respect and wants to behave respectably.* Proof: This follows directly from Theorem 5.1.14 and Axiom 3.7.12.

Theorem 5.1.14.b *Everyone believes that everyone believes that everyone wants to be treated with respect and wants to behave respectably.* Proof: This follows directly from Theorem 5.1.14 and Axiom 3.7.12.

Theorem 5.1.14.c *Everyone believes that everyone believes that everyone believes that everyone wants to be treated with respect and wants to behave respectably.* Proof: This follows directly from Theorem 5.1.14 and Axiom 3.7.12.

Note 3.7.14 The hall of mirrors effect of Axiom 3.7.12 (Smedslund, 1989) enhances the predictability of behavior tremendously. Not only does the axiom facilitate the prediction of individual behavior, but it also enables us to predict complex interactions of many people, under the simplifying assumption that everyone assumes that everyone relies on the self-evident propositions of psychological common sense.

Note 3.7.15 In summary: Wants and beliefs are the main determinants of personal activity. They are primitive terms in the system. Both wants and beliefs may be reflective or unreflective and vary in strength. Persons want to feel good and want not to feel bad. They want to believe what is the case, that is, what is consistent with everything else that is the case. They want to not believe what is not the case. There are no limits to what persons can want and believe, but there are some things everyone wants and everyone believes. Finally, persons assume that self-evident propositions and their implications are shared by everyone, that everyone assumes that they are shared by everyone, and so on.

Chapter 4

Feeling

Note 4.0.0 Feel has already been introduced as a primitive term (2.4.3). It refers to a general aspect of awareness, just as do want and belief. Its usage in ordinary language includes reference to bodily sensations, as in "the water feels cold." It may also refer to the entire body of an individual, as in "I feel cold." Both examples refer to bodily sensations rather than to states of the person. On the other hand, "I feel good" refers to a state of a person and describes what is also called an emotion. Both in ordinary language and in psychological literature, feeling and emotion are often used as synonyms. Hence, a choice of term is necessary. The term feeling is used here, but only in its sense of referring to the state of a person (emotion), and not as referring to bodily sensations.

4.1 *General Characteristics of Feelings*

Note 4.1.0 Feeling is logically related to want and belief. The criteria for characterizing a person's feelings at a given moment are to be found in the relationship between the person's wants and beliefs at that moment. Knowing what a person wants and believes at a given time allows us to infer what the person feels at that time. Bodily and mental symptoms of feeling are also interpreted in the light of this relationship between wants and beliefs. The reader is reminded of the distinction between criteria and symptoms. Criteria are necessary, and taken together, sufficient indicators of the presence of a member of a category. Symptoms are empirically established probabilistic indicators, to be validated against the criteria. Wants and beliefs taken together are the necessary and sufficient criteria of feelings, whereas bodily and mental indicators are empirical symptoms. You *believe* there are burglars in the house and that they will harm you. You *want* not to be harmed. Hence, you *feel* afraid. Your heart rate, perspiration, way of acting, and so on, are *symptoms* of your fear.

Axiom 4.1.1 *P's feeling follows from P's awareness of the relationship between P's wants and P's beliefs.*

Note 4.1.2 Axiom 4.1.1 means that to any given combination of wants and beliefs there corresponds a feeling. How shall a feeling be described? It has already

45

been asserted that in principle, there are no limits to what a person may want and believe. Wants and beliefs are described in terms of what is wanted and what is believed. It follows from this and from Axiom 4.1.1 that there are also no limits to what a person can feel, and that the exact content of the feeling may be described only by reference to the wants and beliefs involved. In the example with the burglars, the person's feeling can be described as "I believed they were going to harm me. I did not want to be harmed, but I did not believe I could prevent it. I wanted to escape, but I did not know how. I felt like one feels having those beliefs and wants." However, no language describes feelings solely by reference to its component wants and beliefs. In the example used here, the English language offers terms such as *afraid* to characterize the person's feeling. I discuss the problems of classification of feelings later in the chapter.

4.2 *Reflectivity of Feelings*

Note 4.2.0 Feelings may be unreflective or reflective. In the former case, they may only be inferred from knowledge of the relationship between the person's wants and beliefs, or probabilistically, from observable symptoms. In the latter case, they may also be talked about by the person.

Definition 4.2.1 "*P has a reflective feeling*" = df "*P has a feeling, and P is aware THAT P has it.*"

Definition 4.2.2 "*P has an unreflective feeling*" = df "*P has a feeling and P is not aware THAT P has it.*"

Corollary 4.2.3 If P has a reflective feeling, then P can talk about that feeling. Proof: This follows directly from Axiom 1.4.11.

Corollary 4.2.4 If P can talk about a feeling, then P has a reflective feeling. Proof: This follows directly from Axiom 1.4.11.

Corollary 4.2.5 If P has an unreflective feeling, then P cannot talk about that feeling. Proof: This follows directly from Axiom 1.4.11.

Corollary 4.2.6 If P cannot talk about a feeling, then P has an unreflective feeling. Proof: This follows directly from Axiom 1.4.11.

Note 4.2.7 Corollaries 4.2.3, 4.2.4, 4.2.5, and 4.2.6 together are equivalent to Axiom 1.4.11, as it applies to feelings.

Note 4.2.8 Because P is the one who has the feeling, it makes no sense, in the terminology used here, to state that P is unaware of P's feeling. The feelings exist for the person and are an aspect of the person's awareness. However, P may not be aware *that* P has these feelings and hence, the awareness may only be unreflective.

Again, the distinction between criteria and symptoms is important. An unreflective feeling may be expressed in various bodily and behavioral symptoms, but the interpretation of these symptoms must rely on the criteria of the feeling. Only if a given relationship between wants and beliefs is known to be present, can a given set of bodily and behavioral symptoms be interpreted as reflecting a particular feeling.

Note 4.2.9 Labeling a person's feelings yields some practically useful information even in the absence of a detailed knowledge of the constituent wants and beliefs. Knowledge about what kind of feeling is involved has at least threefold utility to an observer. First, it informs about the relation between the person who has the feeling and the observer. Second, it informs about the relation between the person and whatever is the target of the feeling. Finally, it informs about the relation between the observer and the target. Example: P declares "I am afraid." This invites O to help P and to calm P. It tells O that P perceives a threat which P does not know if P can cope with. Finally, it alerts O to a possible danger not only to P, but also to O. Similarly, each kind of feeling evokes a characteristic pattern of expectations.Hence, feeling names represent a convenient way of ordering the infinitely variable want/belief relations in a simplified and practically useful way.

4.3. Strength of Feelings

Axiom 4.3.0 *The strength of a feeling is equal to the product of the strength of the want and the strength of the belief, whose relationship constitutes the feeling.*

Note 4.3.1 The strength of feelings, wants and beliefs can, at best, be measured only in ordinal scales. They change constantly and are hard to compare across contexts and over time. Consequently, only certain very crude predictions may be derived from Axiom 4.3.0. W = strength of want, B = strength of belief, and F = strength of feeling.

Corollary 4.3.2 *If $W1 > W2$ and $B1 > B2$, or if $W1 = W2$ and $B1 > B2$, or if $W1 > W2$ and $B1 = B2$, then $F1 = (W1 \times B1) > F2 = (W2 \times B2)$.* Proof: This follows directly from Axiom 4.3.0.

Corollary 4.3.3 *If $F1 = (W1 \times B1) > F2 = (W2 \times B2)$ and $W1 < W2$, then $B1 > B2$.* Proof: This follows directly from Axiom 4.3.0.

Corollary 4.3.4 *If $F1 = (W1 \times B1) > F2 = (W2 \times B2)$ and $B1 < B2$, then $W1 > W2$.* Proof: This follows directly from Axiom 4.3.0.

Note 4.3.5 These corollaries contain some of the implications of the multiplicative function, $F = W \times B$. The happiness on being informed that one has won \$2,000 is stronger than the happiness on being informed that one has won $1,000, if the trustworthiness of the former information is taken to be at least as high as the trustworthiness of the latter information. The relative strength of happiness becomes less predictable when the information that one has won $2,000 is seen as somewhat doubtful, whereas the information about having won $1,000 is taken to be fairly certain, and so on.

Note 4.3.6 Another way of expressing the preceding is to say that the strength of a feeling is directly and monotonically related to the strength of the corresponding want, when the corresponding belief is held constant, and to the corresponding belief when the corresponding want is held constant.

In what follows, the constituent wants and beliefs of feeling X are labeled respectively W(X) and B(X), and the constituent wants and beliefs of feeling Y are labeled respectively W(Y) and B(Y).

Theorem 4.3.7 *"When P's feelings X and Y are in conflict, and no other factors intervene, X is stronger than Y, if, and only if, P tries to act in accordance with X and not in accordance with Y."* Proof: (i) If X is stronger than Y, then, according to Axiom 4.3.0, W(X) x B(X) > W(Y) x B(Y). But, according to Axiom 3.3.2, the strength of a want is proportional to the amount of increment in positive or decrement in negative value expected when the goal is attained, and according to Axiom 3.5.1, the strength of a belief is directly proportional to P's estimate of the likelihood of achieving the goal. Hence, the strength of a feeling is proportional to the expected utility of acting according to that feeling, as given in Definition 2.4.10 (as equal to the product of the expected outcome value of the act and the expected likelihood of the act leading to that outcome). But, according to Corollary 2.4.12, P tries to act according to what has the highest expected utility, in this case according to X and not according to Y. Hence, if X is stronger than Y, then P tries to act in accordance with X and not in accordance with Y. (ii) If P tries to act in accordance with X and not in accordance with Y, then, according to Corollary 2.4.12, acting in accordance with X involves higher expected utility than acting in accordance with Y. But, according to Definition 2.4.10 (of expected utility as product of strength of belief and strength of want) and axiom 4.3.0 (the strength of a feeling is a product of the strengths of the constituent belief and want), expected utility and strength of a feeling are directly proportional. Hence, because acting according to X has higher expected utility than acting according to Y, X is stronger than Y. From (i) and (ii) the theorem follows.

Definition 4.3.8 *"P's feelings A and B are in conflict"* = df *"The wants and the beliefs constituting A and the wants and beliefs constituting B lead to incompatible acts."*

Note 4.3.9 Application of Theorem 4.3.7: In a situation in which fear would lead P to run, whereas pride would lead P to stay (and avoid shame), running or staying indicates which feeling is strongest.

Corollary 4.3.10 *If P has a reflective feeling F, and, if P judges P's ratings of the strength of F to be adequate, then P's ratings of the strength of F will be directly and monotonically related to the actual strength of F.* Proof: It follows from Axiom 1.4.32 that if P judges P's ratings of the strength of F to be adequate, then P's ratings will be correct. But, if they are correct, they must be directly and monotonically related to what is rated. Hence, the corollary is proved.

Note 4.3.11 Axiom 4.3.0, Theorem 4.3.7 and Corollary 4.3.10 indicate three different ways of gauging the strength of a feeling. These involve the product of the strengths of the wants and beliefs constituting the feeling, its dominance over other feelings in determining choice of action, and direct ratings by the person involved. The last method is only available in the case of reflective feelings. The joint implications of these methods may be formulated in the following three theorems:

Theorem 4.3.12 *When P's feelings F1 and F2, are in conflict, P tries to act in accordance with F1 and not in accordance with F2, if, and only if, the product of the strengths of the wants and beliefs constituting F1 is greater than the product of the strengths of the wants and beliefs constituting F2.* Proof: This follows directly from Axiom 4.3.0 and Theorem 4.3.7.

Theorem 4.3.13 *When P's reflective feelings F1 and F2 are in conflict, P tries to act in accordance with F1 and not in accordance with F2, if, and only if, P rates F1 as being stronger than F2."* Proof: This follows directly from Theorem 4.3.7 and Corollary 4.3.10.

Theorem 4.3.14 *The product of the strengths of the want and the belief constituting P's reflective feeling F1 is greater than the product of the strengths of the want and the belief constituting P's reflective feeling F2, if, and only if, P rates F1 as stronger than F2."* Proof: This follows directly from Axiom 4.3.0 and Corollary 4.3.10.

4.4 Categorization of Feelings

Note 4.4.0 Although a given feeling may, in principle, be described exclusively in terms of the constituent wants and beliefs (Note 4.1.2), all languages also have a vocabulary referring to *kinds* of feelings, and these categorizations have obvious utility (Note 4.2.9). However, the task of systematizing the terms for feelings is extraordinarily difficult, both because the meanings of the terms are vague, complex, and partly overlapping, and because different languages have different vocabularies.

Note 4.4.1 The numerous words for feelings in natural languages come in big clusters, with obviously overlapping meanings. For the purpose of systematic analysis, one needs to select a set of terms for feelings which are nonoverlapping in meaning, or in other words, are conceptually independent. The test for conceptual independence goes as follows: Assuming that P has or does not have feeling A, does it follow necessarily from this that P also has or does not have feeling B, and vice versa? If nothing follows either way, then the conclusion is that A and B are conceptually independent of each other. Examples: Suppose that P is happy or unhappy. Does it follow necessarily from either of these that P is delighted or not delighted? And conversely, does it follow necessarily from P is delighted or not delighted that P is happy or unhappy? The answer is clearly that one cannot be happy without being at all delighted and one cannot be delighted without being at all happy. Similarly, it does not make sense to say that someone is totally unhappy but delighted, or not at all delighted, yet happy. The conclusion is that these terms are not conceptually independent. Consider now the pair of terms angry and ashamed: If someone is angry or not angry it does not follow necessarily that he or she is also ashamed or not ashamed. Similarly, if someone is ashamed or not ashamed, it does not follow necessarily that he or she is angry or not angry. Hence, these two terms appear to be conceptually independent. The impressionistic method used here to assess conceptual independence may be improved on in two ways. One is to study the extent to which informants actually treat the concepts as independent, given concrete examples. The other is to provide strict, but generally acceptable, definitions of the concepts and investigate their formal logical relationships.

Note 4.4.2 An exhaustive taxonomy of beliefs has never been seriously proposed, probably because of the obvious lack of constraints involved. Given suitable circumstances a person can believe anything (3.4.5). The same is true of wants (3.1.4), although there have been attempts to construct taxonomies, for example, of the so-called instincts. These efforts ended in absurdity (the thumb-twiddling instinct and the not-thumb-twiddling instinct). Although there are certain universal wants such as those connected with water and food, life allows for the development of literally any kind of want.

Even though the variety of possible feelings is also unlimited, the situation when it comes to classifying them differs from what is the case with beliefs and wants. Whereas understanding a person's beliefs and wants requires knowledge of the specific things believed and wanted, feelings can, as we have already seen, be responded to, at least in a preliminary way, without knowing the details involved (cf. Note 4.2.9). Sadness invites attempts to console, fear invites attempts to protect, anger invites defensiveness, and so on. In general, each kind of feeling involves characteristic demands on the other person. These demands can, to some extent, be responded to in advance of knowledge of the specific wants and beliefs involved. In summary, feelings allow for a taxonomy because they invite a limited number of common response-types.

Note 4.4.3 Mixing of feelings should not be confused with conceptual dependence. It makes sense to talk about mixed feelings, only when the components are conceptually independent. A person can be said to be half ashamed and half angry, precisely because these feelings are conceptually independent. On the other hand, it makes no sense to say that a person is half happy and half delighted. These terms overlap in meaning.

Note 4.4.4 The terminology of mixing of feelings implies a constraint on total capacity for feeling. One can be half angry and half ashamed, but one cannot be maximally angry and maximally ashamed at the same time. This means that increasing one emotion may be a way of decreasing another. Making someone very angry makes that person less anxious, and vice versa. This may be formalized as follows:

Axiom 4.4.5 *The sum of the strengths of a person's feelings at a given moment has an upper limit equal to the maximum possible strength of any single feeling at that moment.*

Note 4.4.6 Since our measures of the strength of feelings are usually very crude, only a few general implications may be drawn from Axiom 4.4.5. Two of the most frequently used of these are as follows:

Corollary 4.4.7 *If the strength of a feeling at a given moment is maximal, then the person can have only that one feeling at that moment.*   P r o o f : This follows directly from Axiom 4.4.5.

Corollary 4.4.8 *If the sum of the strengths of a person's feelings at a given moment is close to maximal, then an increase in the strength of one of the feelings will be accompanied by a decrease in the strength of one or several of the others.*   Proof: This follows directly from Axiom 4.4.5.

Note 4.4.9 A major distinction is between positive and negative feelings. The former involve feeling good and the latter involve feeling bad. In ordinary language, there is a sharp distinction between feeling as a personal state (an emotion) and feeling as a bodily experience. For example, P may taste a good dessert, while being depressed, and may have a tooth ache while being jubilantly happy. Feelings, as used here, are global states involving the *whole* person, whereas pleasures and pains are more or less localized.

4.5 *Positive Feelings*

Note 4.5.0 It is difficult to subdivide the positive feelings in such a way that each resulting category is conceptually independent of all of the others. At least for the time being this effort has been abandoned, and only positive feeling in general, here labeled *happiness*, is included.

Axiom 4.5.1 *P is happy, if, and only if, and to the extent that, P believes that at least one of P's wants is being, or is going to be, fulfilled.*

Note 4.5.2 Happiness is determined by the person's wants and beliefs at a given moment. Since it is linked to fulfillment of wants it is linked to a process and not to a state.

Corollary 4.5.3 *P's degree of happiness is directly proportional to the product of the strength of the want involved and the subjective likelihood of fulfillment of this want."* Proof: This follows directly from Axiom 4.3.0.

Note 4.5.4 Axiom 4.5.1 links happiness to belief in the fulfillment of a want. This makes it meaningful to talk about illusory or mistaken happiness, because the belief may be wrong. Corollary 4.5.3 asserts that the degree of happiness is directly proportional to the product of the strength of the want and the strength of the belief. However, this is only an ideal model. Rarely, if ever, can we measure wants and beliefs on advanced scales. As has been pointed out earlier, products of ordinally measured variables involve some consequences, mostly in the form of predictions about the outcome of certain paired comparisons (cf. Corollaries 4.3.2, 4.3.3, and 4.3.4, dealing with the relative strength of a feeling as a function of the relative strengths of the beliefs and wants involved. These also apply to the degree of happiness).

Note 4.5.5 It is common knowledge that happiness is transitory under many conditions. This has to do with the link to fulfillment of a want. A want is fulfilled within a limited time span, and as it is fulfilled it also diminishes in strength and weakens. This may be expressed in the following theorem:

Theorem 4.5.6 *Other things equal, the amount of happiness reaches a maximum at the onset of a believed certainty of fulfillment of a want, and then diminishes toward zero.* Proof: According to Corollary 4.5.3, P's degree of happiness is directly proportional to the product of the strength of P's want and the subjective likelihood of fulfillment of the want. It follows from this that the degree of happiness reaches a maximum at the moment when the strength of the want has not yet started to diminish, but when the subjective likelihood has turned into certainty. This is the moment when the product of the strengths of the belief and the want reaches a maximum. After this, the fulfillment leads to a decrease of the want. But, a decrease of the want also leads to a decrease of the product of the strengths of want and belief, and, therefore, of happiness. By this, the theorem is proved.

Note 4.5.7 Cases of apparently lasting happiness may seem to pose a problem for the present position. However, several types of interpretation are possible. Some recurrent postachievement happiness may be mediated by recalling the achievement of the goal and the happiness associated with it. Alleged cases of stable happiness often involve global characterizations of a person's life over a period of time. When closely inspected, this may involve continuously occurring and often recurrent fulfillments of many wants, each of which instigates some transitory happiness as postulated by Theorem 4.5.6.

Note 4.5.8 The transitory character of happiness is a fundamental aspect of human life, and poses a constant strategic problem. How shall one organize one's life in order to generate as much happiness as possible? Not only is the fulfillment of a want followed by diminishing happiness, but repeated fulfillments of the same want under the same circumstances often seems to weaken the want and hence, the happiness generated.

Some further explications of implicitly known circumstances may be possible here, for example regarding the quest for novelty as a source of new happiness.

4.6 Negative Feelings

Note 4.6.0 It is possible to discern among the numerous English terms designating negative feelings, a set of at least nine feelings, which can be regarded as conceptually independent of each other. These are *boredom, anger, fear, shame, guilt, sadness, envy, suspiciousness,* and *disgust.* This list is tentative and may, perhaps, be lengthened. It represents an attempt to systematize some core distinctions in the vocabulary of the English language. Other natural languages may yield partly different lists. However, all of the feelings suggested here are characterized by a particular relationship between the person's wants and beliefs, hence conforming with Axiom 4.1.1. They include the negative feelings listed by Lazarus (1991), and in addition, boredom and suspiciousness.

Axiom 4.6.1 *P is bored if, and only if, P believes that P cannot act toward any of P's goals, and cannot leave the situation for some time.*

Corollary 4.6.2 *The strength of P's boredom is directly proportional to the degree of absence of possibilities for meaningful action, including the expected duration of the absence.*   Proof: This follows directly from Axiom 4.6.1 and Axiom 4.3.0.

Note 4.6.3 A boring situation is one in which there is nothing meaningful to do, yet one does not want to leave. The reason why there is nothing to do is that there is nothing in the situation one wants or believes is relevant for something one wants. It is important that the boring situation is seen as temporary. If the situation were seen to be permanent, there would be attempts to escape, and a whole range of possible other negative feelings, depending on the particular circumstances (see later).

People are susceptible to boredom to varying degrees. The differences reflect their wants and beliefs and their ability to extract or create interesting tasks out of seemingly barren situations. Folk psychology has rich intuitions in this area, especially in connection with waiting rooms. Usually such rooms are provided with pictures on the walls, a rich supply of magazines, and maybe background music. When these props are insufficient, people try to engage in planning, daydreaming, or conversation.

Axiom 4.6.4 *P is angry at O, if, and only if, P believes that at least one person whom P cares for has, intentionally or through neglect, been treated without respect by O, and P has not forgiven O.*

Note 4.6.5 To be treated with respect is further discussed in chapter 5. It means being accorded the basic rights and duties one is entitled to. This may include being treated justly, politely, considerately, and also being expected to be just, polite, and considerate oneself. Believed lack of respect is the occasion for anger, which also includes a want to *retaliate*. This essentially means to try to *force* the other one to apologize and to become respectful again ("get even"). Indignation is a word for anger when it is felt to be particularly well morally justified.

Note 4.6.6 People differ in the amount and kind of respect they feel entitled to, and in the amount and kind of respect they think particular others are entitled to (Smedslund, 1993). The differences may be idiosyncratic, or they may be linked with cultural differences in how factors such as age, title, wealth, caste, accomplishments, and so on, determine what is regarded as appropriately respectful behavior.

Corollary 4.6.7 *The strength of P's anger is directly proportional to the product of the subjective likelihood of, and the amount of, disrespect P believes has been shown.* Proof: This follows directly from Axiom 4.6.4 and Axiom 4.3.0 (The strength of a feeling is equal to the product of the strength of the want and the strength of the belief whose relationship constitutes the feeling.)

Note 4.6.8 Anger should not be confused with aggression, which is acting intended to inflict pain and harm. Although anger is often expressed through aggressive acts, there is no necessary link between them. You may act aggressively without being angry, either in order to fake anger, or for other reasons. For example, a soldier may act under orders to kill and destroy, while feeling only disgust and/or guilt at what he is doing. One may also be angry without displaying aggression, because it is not regarded as prudent to do so. For example, acting aggressively may be regarded as too dangerous, or in some other way unwise.

Theorem 4.6.9 *If P is angry, then P is frustrated.* Proof: According to Axiom 4.6.4, if P is angry, then P believes someone P cares for has been treated with disrespect. But, because P believes that people ought to be treated with respect and, because, according to Axiom 1.3.11, P wants everyone to accept what P believes is right, it follows that P is frustrated.

Note 4.6.10 Theorem 4.6.9 is the only valid part of the original frustration/aggression hypothesis.

Axiom 4.6.11 *P is afraid, if, and only if, P believes that, regardless of what P does, there is a definite possibility that P will be harmed.*

Note 4.6.12 The preceding axiom states that there is a believed danger and that one's personal powers are believed to be insufficient to avert it. From this it follows that, other things equal, the weaker a person sees him or herself, the more frequently will that person be afraid. It also follows that persons who tend to see the world as full of dangers will be more often afraid than those who see few dangers.

Corollary 4.6.13 *Other things equal, the weaker P believes P is, the more frequently will P be afraid.*   Proof: This follows directly from Axiom 4.6.11.

Corollary 4.6.14 *Other things equal, the more often P believes there is danger, the more often will P be afraid.*   Proof: This follows directly from Axiom 4.6.11.

Axiom 4.6.17 *P feels ashamed, if, and only if, P believes that P has done something which P ought not to have done, either because it is regarded as unseemly, or because it was done incompetently.*

Note 4.6.18 Shame is the feeling one has when one's performance and appearance deviates from what one regards as acceptable standards. The ashamed person believes that others see him or her as ridiculous, and fears being ridiculed. A person who is particularly afraid of ridicule may become unusually *shy* or unusually *aggressive*. By being shy P has a chance of avoiding attention and, hence, ridicule, and by being aggressive, P has a chance of scaring others from ridiculing P.

Corollary 4.6.19 *The strength of P's shame is directly proportional to the product of the likelihood of, and the amount of, ridicule P believes is involved* Proof: This follows directly from Axiom 4.6.17 and Axiom 4.3.0.

Note 4.6.20 A person's shame is stronger the more important the observers are in his or her life, that is, the more their opinions make a difference for him or her. The display of unseemly or incompetent behavior to complete strangers, that is, to people who do not know you and whom you will never see again, creates comparatively little shame. Conversely, when you are very ashamed of something you have done and this is known to everyone in your surroundings, it may be a very heavy burden to live with. Shame is a feeling centering on oneself as one believes others see one.

Axiom 4.6.21 *P feels guilt towards O, if, and only if, P believes that P has done something wrong to O and has not been forgiven.*

Note 4.6.22 Guilt always has to do with wrongdoing against one or more *persons*. It may be one particular person, a group of persons, people in a country, people in general, oneself, God, or a pet or other animal. In the latter cases, God and the animals are seen as having personlike characteristics, such as being aware, being capable of suffering, being able to feel rejected and maltreated, being capable of love, and so on.

Note 4.6.23 Persons differ greatly in the prominence of guilt feelings in their lives. This must be related, on the one hand, to the severity of their own norms and their ensuing tendency to transgress them, and on the other hand, to their tendency to blame themselves rather than other people or the circumstances.

Corollary 4.6.24 *Other things equal, the more severe and all-encompassing P's normative beliefs, the more frequently P will suffer from feelings of guilt.* Proof: This follows directly from Axiom 4.6.21.

Corollary 4.6.25 *Other things equal, the stronger P's tendency to assume responsibility for outcomes of interaction with others, the more frequently P will suffer from feelings of guilt.* Proof: This follows directly from Axiom 4.6.21

Note 4.6.26 Guilt feelings are characterized by being difficult to change because they concern something past and hence, are irrevocable. Only a few alternatives are open for the sufferer of guilt. In a few cases, it may be possible to, literally, undo the deed, and even obliterate all traces of it. In other cases, you may offer compensations and consolations of various sorts to the victim. You may also undergo self-imposed or legally imposed penalties that may be seen as having a cleansing effect. You have suffered your punishment and now you have a clean conscience again. Finally, you may ask to be forgiven. Genuine forgiving may be felt like a blessing, but there are always doubts, and the board may never be wiped entirely clean. Some record is usually kept and newborn saints are still have-been sinners (Smedslund, 1991a).

Corollary 4.6.27 *The strength of P's feeling of guilt is directly proportional to the product of the likelihood of and the severity of, the wrongdoing that P believes is involved.* Proof: This follows directly from Axiom 4.6.21 and Axiom 4.3.0.

Axiom 4.6.28 *P is sad, if, and only if, P believes that something P wants has become irrevocably lost.*

Note 4.6.29 Sadness involves a belief that something wanted will forever remain unattainable. It also involves a *passivity*, reflecting the belief that nothing can be done. Crying is a universal expression of sadness (grief, sorrow). Because all activity is intentional it must be assumed that crying has the goal of evoking sympathy, compassion, support, and so on. Under circumstances where sympathy is not forthcoming one may expect crying to be rare.

Corollary 4.6.30 *The strength of sadness is equal to the product of the strength of the frustrated want and the strength of the belief that what is wanted is lost.* Proof: This follows directly from Axiom 4.3.0.

Note 4.6.31 There is a particular variant of sadness that has to do with a person's total life situation and that may be labelled *depression*. A person may be sad because of something that has been lost, but this feeling will normally diminish after a while.

However, if the sadness has to do with a stable and apparently unchangeable total life situation or with faults in one's own personality, it is likely to persevere for longer periods of time.

Axiom 4.6.32 *P is depressed, if, and only if, P believes that P's lot can never be improved in the way P wants it to be, and/or P can never become the sort of person P wants to be.*

Note 4.6.33 It can be seen from Axioms 4.6.28 and 4.6.32 that depression is a subclass of sadness. Hence, if a person is depressed then he or she is sad, but a person may be sad without being depressed.

Note 4.6.34 Depression may also develop in persons living under conditions of endemic poverty, hunger and unemployment. Here, it is attributed to conditions beyond the power of individuals to change. Depression is also frequent in periods of human life where great changes are taking place. In young people there may be depression because they believe that they are unable to become the persons they would like to be. They believe they do not have and never will have the looks, the charm, the abilities, the opportunities, that they would like to have. In old age, there may be depression because of irreversible loss of health, physical and mental agility, attractiveness, possibilities, and so on.

Axiom 4.6.35 *P is envious of O, if, and only if, P wants to have something that P believes O has, and/or wants O not to have it.*

Note 4.6.36 Envy is not regarded as a nice feeling, because it may lead to immoral acts of taking things away from other persons. It depends on a belief that the other person has things you yourself want and do not have. Frequently, the envy may be morally justified by the argument that the other one does not deserve what he or she has, whereas you deserve to have it. Under some circumstances envy may be purely negative. One wants O not to have something, and taking it away from O satisfies the envious want.

Corollary 4.6.37 *The strength of envy is equal to the product of the strength of the want to have what the other has, and the strength of the belief that the other one has it.* Proof: This follows directly from Axiom 4.3.0.

Note 4.6.38 *Jealousy* is often listed as a basic negative feeling. It is not included here, because it involves resentment and hence, is not conceptually independent of anger. In the present exhaustive and exclusive categorization, jealousy is therefore, regarded as a composite feeling.

Axiom 4.6.39 *P is suspicious, if, and only if, P believes that something may not be what it appears to be, and that this discrepancy is intentional.*

Note 4.6.40 Although the term *suspicious* is used in many content areas, its main application is in the domain of interpersonal relations. Suspicion is the feeling aroused when the possibility is entertained that other persons are intentionally deceiving you, lying, faking, simulating, manipulating, and so on. If others are thought to cooperate in doing this, the term "conspiracy" applies. Highly suspicious persons find many occasions for doubting the sincerity of what is socially expressed.

Note 4.6.41 The feeling of being suspicious is constituted, on the one hand, by a want to believe what is the case (Axiom 3.6.2), and the ensuing intolerance of ambiguity (Theorem 3.6.7). On the other hand, the feeling is constituted by a belief that there is intentional deceit. This means that all attempts to determine what is the case are expected to be obstructed.

Axiom 4.6.42 *P is disgusted with X, if, and only if, P is in contact with X, and this is incompatible with P's moral and/or esthetic and/or hygienic standards.*

Note 4.6.43 The feeling of disgust (revulsion) is clearly related to some notion of cleanliness or pollution. It has to do with being a decent person and responding aversely to what is indecent and outside the boundaries of what is acceptable. There are socially imposed standards of personal hygiene, eating and drinking habits, sexual behavior, religious behavior, and so on. The more blatant the deviations from these standards, the stronger one's disgust. Although the metaphors relating to disgust clearly have to do with the body, the feeling of disgust can be as prominent in reactions to, for example, political or religious messages.

Note 4.6.44 Interpersonally, disgust is associated with wholesale rejection of a person. It may well be that the message of tolerance in modern society masks a lot of disgust. Complete tolerance would turn people into caricatures and society into chaos. Socialized individuals always have standards and deviation from these always creates disgust.

Note 4.6.45 In summary, a person's feeling derives from the relationship between the person's wants and the person's beliefs. The person may not be reflectively aware that he or she feels something. A person may at any moment have only one feeling or a mixture of feelings. Feelings are not regarded as separate entities with particular bodily and/or behavioral symptoms, but are simply a convenient way of ordering want-belief relations into frequently occurring categories. Feelings are states of the whole person, whereas pleasure and pain are localized bodily experiences. Positive feelings occur when a person believes that a want is, or is going to be, satisfied. Negative feelings occur when a person believes that a want is, or is going to be, frustrated. Nine conceptually independent negative feelings are described.

Chapter 5

Interpersonal Processes

Note 5.0.0 The preceding chapters have provided concepts for analyzing the processes in individual persons. The key concepts are *wants, beliefs, feelings, abilities*, and *acts*. A person is constantly integrating his or her beliefs into a single view of the situation, and integrating his or her wants into a single plan for what he or she wants to achieve at this point. At each moment, these views and plans give rise to a feeling state and to acting, within the limits of the person's abilities. The existence at each moment of a unitary, integrated state makes it possible for other persons to monitor and respond to what is going on.

Note 5.0.1 The preceding account of a person's processes is incomplete. It treats a person as a nonsocial being seen by an unengaged scientific observer. What is lacking is an explicit recognition of the fact that persons are social beings. They develop and live in constant interaction with others and can only be known through an *encounter*. Hence, the next step is to describe the psychologic of interpersonal processes. At this level of analysis, the key concepts are *respect, care, understanding, control*, and *trust*.

5.1. Respect

Note 5.1.0 The primitive terms *right* (1.3.0) and *wrong* (1.3.1) have already been introduced. They are used to formally define the term *respect*.

Definition 5.1.1 "*P respects O*" = df "*P regards O as someone who ought to be treated rightly.*"

Definition 5.1.2 "*P treats O with respect*" = df "*P treats O rightly.*"

Corollary 5.1.3 *If P treats O without respect, then P treats O wrongly.*
Proof: This follows directly from Definition 5.1.2.

Note 5.1.4 To be treated rightly, that is, with respect, means to be treated according to one's societally defined rights. Other frequent words for this are considerately, correctly, courteously, politely, and justly. The specific rules making up the concrete content of respect vary from one culture to another. In contemporary Western societies, the right to have an autonomous private life is much emphasized, as is the basically egalitarian status of individuals.

Note 5.1.5 Respect is an attitude of P toward O which, normally but not always, results in P actually treating O with respect. A number of implications of the two definitions serve as guidelines in everyday life, and characterize the relationship between the attitude and the corresponding action.

Theorem 5.1.6 *If P respects O, then P wants to treat O with respect.*
Proof: If P respects O, then, according to Definition 5.1.1, P regards O as someone who ought to be treated rightly. But, if P believes that O ought to be treated rightly, then according to Axiom 1.3.9 (P wants to do what P believes is right, and wants not to do what P believes is wrong), P wants to treat O rightly, that is, wants to treat O with respect.

Note 5.1.7 Even though as stated in the preceding theorem, respecting a person implies wanting to treat that person respectfully, the realization of that want only occurs under certain conditions, specified in the psychologic of action (see chapter 2).

Corollary 5.1.8 *P treats O with respect, if, and only if, P can treat O with respect and P tries to treat O with respect.*   Proof: This follows directly from Axiom 2.2.3 (P does A, if, and only if, P can do A and P tries to do A).

Note 5.1.9 The preceding corollary indicates two possible reasons why P may not treat O with respect, even though P respects O and wants to treat O with respect. One possible reason is that P cannot treat O with respect and another possible reason is that P does not try. The conditions of trying to treat with respect are given in the following corollary:

Corollary 5.1.10 *P tries to treat O with respect, if, and only if, treating O with respect has the highest expected utility for P.*   Proof: This follows directly from Corollary 2.4.12 (P tries to do A, if, and only if, A is the act which, for P, has the highest expected utility).

Note 5.1.11 Because expected utility is defined as the product of the expected value of the outcome and the expected likelihood of achieving that outcome, it can be seen that there is no necessary link between wanting to treat someone with respect and trying to do so. The reason is that, even though strength of want is directly proportional to the expected goal value (Axiom 3.3.2), there may be no trying if the subjective likelihood of goal achievement is zero and consequently, the expected utility is zero, or if the expected utility of another (nonrespectful) act is higher than the expected utility of acting respectfully.

Note 5.1.12 As with every other attitude, respect may be simulated. To try to simulate respect means that P tries to make O believe that P respects O, whereas P actually does not.

Note 5.1.13 Respect, as defined here, should not be confused with *admiration* for what someone has done, or *awe* for someone's power. Admiration and awe are linked to perceived superiority in personal ability or power. If a person fails to do well or becomes powerless, admiration and awe may change into indifference or even contempt. Respect is linked to membership and status, in a society. In the modern world, all members of the species homo sapiens are taken to be entitled to respectful treatment (human rights). Animal rights movements and many religions also include members of other species. Because respect is connected with membership status, wholesale excommunication means that the individual is no longer entitled to respect.

Theorem 5.1.14 *P wants to be treated with respect and wants to behave respectably.* Proof: According to Definition 5.1.2, to be treated with respect is to be treated rightly. To behave respectably is to treat others rightly. According to Axiom 1.3.11, P wants everyone to accept what P believes is right and to reject what P believes is wrong. From this it follows that P wants everyone to treat everyone rightly. This implies that P wants to be treated rightly, that is, with respect, and wants everyone to behave rightly, that is, respectably. By this the theorem is proved.

Note 5.1.15 It does not contradict the preceding that a person also may want *not* to have a certain status and hence, may want to escape the rights and duties linked with that status. What the person does depends on the relative strength of the various conflicting wants.

Note 5.1.16 If a person does not want to be treated with respect and does not want to behave respectably, then it follows from Axiom 1.3.9 that the person does not believe in the validity of the relevant norms and hence, does not want to be a member of the community in which these norms are taken to be valid. However, there is *always* another real or imagined society, reference group, or reference person from whom the person wants to receive respect, and toward whom the person *wants* to behave respectably.

Axiom 5.1.17 *For every P, there exists at least one O, such that P respects O and P wants O to respect P.*

Note 5.1.18 This axiom reflects the social (dialogical) nature of the person. It shares with most of the axioms of EL the following three characteristics: First, it appears to have face validity in an overwhelming majority of the cases. Second, most isolated individuals have fictional or fantasy figures conforming with the axiom. Finally, the axiom is strongly plausible when seen from the perspective of most conceptions of the self and the person.

Note 5.1.19 To behave respectably is also to behave in a way "worthy of" respect. There is a tendency to think that one "earns" respect and, therefore, it is hard to treat someone with respect who does not behave respectably. On the other hand, there is also a tendency to think that merely being a person, possibly with a certain status, entitles one to be treated with respect irrespective of how one behaves. This dilemma is a recurrent one and can never be finally settled.

Note 5.1.20 The concept of respect reflects the normativity of all psychological processes at the interpersonal level. Everything you do that involves another person has a normative value and hence, expresses respect or disrespect.

5.2 Care

Note 5.2.0 The primitive terms *want* (3.1.1), *feel* (2.4.3), and *good* (2.4.1) have already been introduced. They are used to formally define the term *care*.

Definition 5.2.1 "*P cares for O*" = df "*P wants O to feel good*".

Note 5.2.2 Caring for another person is an all encompassing attitude. It makes little sense to say that one cares for a person with respect to certain matters, but not with respect to others, or that one cares for the person at certain times and not at others. Caring involves the other person as a whole. To be sure, one may begin to care for someone and one may cease to care for someone, but *while* one cares for someone it is a global, that is, generalized, attitude.

Theorem 5.2.3 *If P cares for O, then P wants to keep track of how things go with O.* Proof: According to Definition 5.2.1, if P cares for O, then P wants O to feel good. But in order to know what needs to be done to keep O feeling good, P must keep track of how things go with O.

Theorem 5.2.4 *If P cares for O, then P tries to make O feel good, unless other acts have a higher expected utility for P.* Proof: According to Definition 5.2.1, if P cares for O, then P wants to make O feel good. But, in order to make O feel good, P must try to do so. According to Corollary 2.4.12, P will try to make O feel good, if, and only if, this has the highest expected utility for P. Hence, the theorem is proved.

Theorem 5.2.5 *If P cares for O, then P feels good when O feels good.* Proof: According to Definition 5.2.1, if P cares for O, then P wants O to feel good. But, according to Axiom 3.2.9, a person feels good when the person's want is fulfilled. Hence, the theorem follows.

Theorem 5.2.6 *If P cares for O, then P feels bad when O feels bad.* Proof: According to Definition 5.2.1, if P cares for O, then P wants O to feel good. O feels bad. It follows from Axiom 3.2.1 that if a person's want is not fulfilled then that person feels bad. Hence, P feels bad and the theorem is proved.

Definition 5.2.7 "*P likes O*" = df "*P feels good being with O.*"

Theorem 5.2.8 *If P likes O, then P wants to be with O.* Proof: According to Definition 5.2.7, if P likes O, then P feels good being with O. But, according to Axiom 3.2.1 what persons want is to feel good. It follows that P wants to be with O.

Note 5.2.9 Caring for should not be confused with liking a person, although these typically go together. You may like to be with a person because you think the person is beautiful, sexy, funny, a good listener, entertaining, because he or she likes, understands or cares for *you*, and so on. These are all *egoistic* (selfish) pleasures. On the other hand, care involves concern about the other person's situation, and, hence, is an *altruistic* (unselfish) want. The distinction between liking because one derives pleasure from being with a person, and caring about that person, becomes clear when the person no longer provides pleasure. When the beautiful one gets fat or wrinkled, or when the entertainer gets angry, the liking which is linked only to one's own well-being may diminish, whereas the caring, if there is any, may remain. The ordinary language term "like" blurs this important distinction.

Axiom 5.2.10 *Every person wants to care for someone.*

Note 5.2.11 The preceding axiom does not state that persons always care for someone or act caringly. It only asserts that a want to care for someone always exists. Whether it is manifested in action depends on its strength relative to other wants.

Theorem 5.2.12 *Every person wants to be cared for by someone.*
Proof: O either cares for P, is indifferent toward P, or is hostile toward P. If O is indifferent toward P, then O will do nothing to make P feel good or to prevent P from feeling bad. Because P knows this and because P wants to feel good and to avoid feeling bad, P must want O not to be indifferent. Similarly, if O is hostile toward P, then O will try to make P feel bad. Because P knows this, and because P wants to feel good and to avoid feeling bad, P must want O not to be hostile. Because P wants O not to be indifferent and not to be hostile, it follows that P must want O to care for P.

Note 5.2.13 The frequent occurrence of persons living more or less without any caring relationships need not be taken to weaken the plausibility of Axiom 5.2.10 and Theorem 5.2.12. First, one may want to escape from isolation without being able to do so. In order to try, there must be no other want or combination of wants stronger than the want to be cared for and to care for. We know that there often are stronger wants, for example, to avoid being rejected and ridiculed. Second, even if the fear of rejection is overcome, and the person tries to get out of the isolation, this may fail because of external circumstances (task difficulty) and/or because of lack of ability (social skill).

Note 5.2.14 The widespread practice of keeping pets is consistent with Axiom 5.2.10 and Theorem 5.2.12. People may care deeply for their pets and often also believe that the pets care for them. However, it appears more plausible to assume that the pet *likes* its caretaker, in the sense of enjoying being with the caretaker.

Note 5.2.15 *Liking* a person, defined as wanting to be *with* a person (Definition 5.2.7), also involves a striving toward reciprocity, which may be expressed as follows:

Theorem 5.2.16 *P wants his or her liking of a person to be reciprocated.*
Proof: According to Definition 5.2.7, P likes O means P wants to be with O. But, P knows that the likelihood of achieving this goal is sharply increased if O likes P and hence, wants to be with P. Therefore, P wants that O wants to be with P, that is, according to Definition 5.2.7, P wants O to like P.

Note 5.2.17 Being cared for is, in itself, a positive situation and something a person wants. This is so because the person's own striving toward feeling good is supported and supplemented by caring other persons. It is also reasonable to assume that, other things equal, the want to be cared for is inversely proportional to one's own powers. The weaker, the poorer, and the more helpless a person is, the more can he or she expect to profit from care, and the stronger will be the want to be helped. Children, old people and ill people are among the obvious candidates for being cared for. However, there are also wants that make a person averse to being cared for. These include a want to be self-reliant, to master problems on one's own. Furthermore, one may want to avoid the frequent negative aspects of being helpless and dependent on another person. If that person does not treat you with respect and understanding, the care may not be appreciated and the outcome may be bad instead of good feelings. Particularly in adolescence, the transition from dependence to independence is fraught with difficulties. Unless the care of the parents is guided by respect and understanding, being cared for may come to be experienced as something negative to be avoided.

5.3 Understanding

Primitive term 5.3.0 *Understand*

**Axiom 5.3.1 *P understands what O means by saying or doing A,
if, and only if, P and O agree as to what, for O, is equivalent to
A, implied by A, contradicted by A, and irrelevant to A.***

Note 5.3.2 Because the set of expressions stating what is equivalent to, implied by, contradicted by, and irrelevant to a given expression is indefinite in size, understanding of what was meant can never be ascertained completely and with certainty. Usually, understanding is only checked as far as it has immediate practical consequences. For a discussion and rejection of alternative analyses of understanding see Smedslund (1990b).

Axiom 5.3.3 *P understands why O does A if, and only if, P and O agree about which wants and beliefs of O are involved in O doing A.*

Note 5.3.4 The set of wants and beliefs of O that are involved in O doing A is indefinite in extension, and agreement is usually checked only with respect to the most salient components. Axioms 5.3.1 and 5.3.3 are about O's reflective wants and beliefs, which can be talked about and agreed on. O's unreflective wants and beliefs, as well as P's unreflective wants and beliefs concerning O are matters that P and O are not aware *that* they are aware of, and hence cannot talk about and agree on. Nevertheless, *tacit* or *implicit* understanding may be revealed by P and O acting *as if* agreeing on what is implied by A, and so on.

Note 5.3.5 Axioms 5.3.1 and 5.3.3 respectively, concern understanding of what is meant by an act and of what initiated an act. The first is understanding of what follows from something and the second is understanding of what something follows from.

Note 5.3.6 Understanding of what is done and of why it is done should not be confused with agreement in beliefs or agreement on values. There is mutual understanding between P and O, about what O meant by doing A, when they agree on what, for O, is equivalent and so on to the given act A, and about what beliefs and wants of O led to A. However, it does not follow from this mutual understanding that they agree about A's truth or A's value, or about what A should properly mean. Understanding is a precondition for, but not identical to, agreement or disagreement about facts (what is the case), values (what is good and bad) or norms (what is right and wrong).

Theorem 5.3.7 *Every person wants to be understood by others and wants to understand others.*   Proof: If a person does not understand others and is not understood by them, no orderly interaction can occur. This follows because without understanding there is no agreement about what is meant by acts and about why they are performed (Axioms 5.3.1 and 5.3.3). Hence, the participants cannot anticipate each others' future actions. But, in order to achieve goals involving interaction with others, the person must be able to anticipate their actions, and they must be able to anticipate his or hers. Therefore, it follows that the person must want to understand and to be understood.

Note 5.3.8 The preceding theorem is *one* way in which the want to understand and to be understood can be proved within the present system. It appears to be as fundamental as the corresponding propositions about respect (5.1.14) and care (5.2.10 and 5.2.12).

Note 5.3.9 It does not follow from Theorem 5.3.7 that everyone *always* tries to make him or herself understood and tries to understand others. According to Corollary 2.4.12, one always tries to perform the act with the highest expected utility. This means that trying to make oneself intelligible and to understand others is restricted to those situations where this appears to be advantageous. Frequently, tendencies to act on the basis of, for example, fear or shame, may inhibit attempts to understand and to make oneself understood.

Note 5.3.10 Because people frequently do *not* try to unveil themselves to others and frequently do *not* try to understand others, and because, according to Theorem 5.3.7, they want to be understood and to understand others, it follows that there must be powerful contrary wants. Some of these are obvious. You want to avoid being punished, ridiculed, rejected, ignored, abused, and so on. Revealing yourself makes you more vulnerable and easier to manipulate. If the other person is malevolent or indifferent, he or she may use the information about you to cause you pain and harm. This may be formulated as follows:

Theorem 5.3.11 *If P believes that O does not care for P, then P will try not to give O information which may be used by O to cause P harm or pain.* Proof: If P believes that O does not care for P, then P must believe that O is either indifferent or hostile to P. If O is indifferent, this means that O may harm P through lack of interest in avoiding harming P, and also through not actively protecting P. If O is hostile to P, O is likely to try to harm P. In both cases it follows that, because P wants to avoid harm, P will try to withhold information from O.

Note 5.3.12 The reason why people often do not try to understand others, even when it is directly relevant for a project at hand, may be that such understanding could give them guilt feelings (in situations where the question is who is guilty), or could threaten their plans and feelings of autonomy (in situations where the question is who is in charge). Another reason is that trying to understand may involve exertion and people want to minimize exertion (Axiom 2.4.7).

Note 5.3.13 Understanding is a necessary condition for a person to function. If a person encounters totally incomprehensible others and is him or herself totally unintelligible to these others, no orderly interaction can ensue. The only solution is a socialization process in which the participants acquire a set of shared meanings.

Note 5.3.14 The acquisition of new understanding always depends on earlier understandings in an open-ended sequence. This may be expressed in the following axiom:

Axiom 5.3.15 *All understanding depends on relevant pre-understanding.*

5.4 *Control*

Definition 5.4.0 *"P controls E"* = df *"P can make E occur and not occur according to P's wants."*

Note 5.4.1 The concept of control is linked to the concepts of can and want. You have control over that which you can make vary according to your wants. Two other closely related terms are *power* and *freedom*.

Theorem 5.4.2 *Every person wants to have control in matters involving the fulfillment of wants.* Proof: According to Definition 5.4.0, control enables a person to fulfill his or her wants. Therefore, every person must want to have control in matters involving the fulfillment of wants.

Note 5.4.3 One may distinguish between personal wants and wants that have to do with obeying norms taken to be valid. These latter wants may be labeled *normative* (cf. Axiom 1.3.9).

Theorem 5.4.4 *Every person wants to have control in matters involving norms taken by that person to be valid.* Proof: According to Axiom 1.3.9, persons want to obey norms they take to be valid. Hence, it follows from Theorem 5.4.2 that they must want to have control in order to ensure their own obedience of valid norms.

Note 5.4.5 Theorem 5.4.4 may also be said to imply that persons want to act in respectable ways, that is, in ways that do not conflict with existing norms. A person who believes that she or he does not have sufficient control in this respect, may ask for help and seek treatment. There are three types of control:

Definition 5.4.6 *"P has own-control of act A"* = df *"P does or does not do A according to P's wants, and independently of the wants of other persons."*

Note 5.4.7 This is a situation in which P can say, "you cannot stop me from doing it," or "you cannot force me to do it." The term *own-control* is new, but describes an important distinction in everyday life.

Definition 5.4.8 *"P has other-control of O's act A"* = df *"P can make O do or not do A, according to P's wants, independently of O's wants."*

Note 5.4.9 Given *other-control* P can say to O, "I decide what you do and don't do," or "I can make you do it," or "I can stop you from doing it." Again, this is a new term, but it corresponds clearly to a distinction made in everyday life. A third kind of control, *self-control*, is treated in the next section and in chapter 6.

Note 5.4.10 There are three main problems of control in every person's life. One is the balance between P's own-control and other persons' control of P. At the one extreme is the completely independent person who can prevent others from influencing him or her in any way. At the other extreme is the person who cannot avoid following any suggestions and orders from others. A second problem is the balance between P's other-control and other persons' own-control. At the one extreme is the dominant person who can direct other persons' behavior in every detail. At the other extreme is the person who cannot in any way interfere with others' behavior. A third problem is the balance between a person's personal and normative wants. At the one extreme is the totally controlled person who never does anything he or she considers to be wrong. At the other extreme is the totally uncontrolled person who lives only according to his or her personal wants and is incapable of normatively based restraint. This last problem has to do with self-control and is further treated in section 5.5 and in chapter 6.

Note 5.4.11 Logically, there are four possible extreme states of control or lack of control that may characterize a person's situation relative to others.

State 1. *High own-control, high other-control* This may be a powerful, domineering person, and/or a person in a superordinate position.

State 2. *High own-control, low other-control* This describes a situation in which a person can do what he or she likes, but has no control of what the other one does. An example could be the interaction of high-ranking officials in two independent organizations, no one having any authority over, or other means of coercing, the other.

State 3. *Low own-control, high other-control* This exemplifies a situation in which a person is cooperating on equal footing with another. Each person is dependent on the other one, and each person can veto any decision. Hence, decisions can only be made through negotiated agreement.

State 4. *Low own-control, low other-control* This is the case of a powerless, weak person, and/or a person in a subordinate position.

Note 5.4.12 The four possible extreme states may be reduced to three types of extreme dyadic interactions between persons. The first type is the master/slave, superordinate/subordinate interaction (*coercion*), the second is the interaction of mutually independent partners (*consultation*), and the third is the interaction of mutually dependent partners (*cooperation*). The superordinate person has high own-control and high other-control, and the subordinate person has correspondingly low own-control and low other-control. Both mutually independent partners have high own-control and low other-control, they cannot control each other. The mutually dependent partners both have low own-control and high other-control, each can stop the other from doing something. It is common to the last two combinations that they can act together only when both agree.

5.5 Trust

Note 5.5.0 The analysis of interpersonal relationships in terms of respect, care, understanding, and own- and other-control, yields, as we have seen, a number of derivations. However, for many practical purposes, one needs to move to an even more complex level of analysis, namely that described by the concept of *trust*. It appears that the presence versus absence of trust is a function of the aforementioned elementary variables (see Theorem 5.5.25).

Note 5.5.1 In nearly all human transactions the participants can hurt each other, that is, are *vulnerable*. Hence, in all formulae of psychologic involving interpersonal processes, it is assumed that P believes that it is *possible* for O to harm P, that is, P feels *vulnerable* when relating to O. This is given the status of axiom.

Axiom 5.5.2 *P believes that O can harm P.*

Note 5.5.3 Axiom 5.5.2 applies to almost all interpersonal transactions. When it does not apply, that is, when P believes that it is impossible for O to harm P in any way, the interpersonal process becomes atypical of ordinary life.

Note 5.5.4 The possibility of O harming P must not be confused with the likelihood of O harming P. The possibility merely refers to what P thinks O *can* do. Hence, to think that one is vulnerable does not imply that one expects to be harmed. Note also that felt vulnerability refers to what a person *believes* the other person can do and must not be confused with what the other person *really* can do.

Definition 5.5.5 "*P trusts O*" = df "*P believes O will not do anything bad to P.*"

Note 5.5.6 In what follows, the necessary and sufficient conditions of trust are derived. Although the dimensions of interpersonal processes already introduced are all important in the establishment and maintenance of trust, they are not always logically independent of each other, and they also need to be supplemented. Specifically, it appears that respect, although a necessary condition of trust, can be derived from care and understanding, and also that a factor of assumed know-how needs to be added. P cannot trust O if P believes that O is incompetent.

Theorem 5.5.7 *If P trusts O, then P believes that O respects P.*   Proof: If P believes that O does not respect P, then P expects to be treated without respect by O. But, according to Theorem 5.1.14 (every person wants to be treated with respect and wants to behave respectably), to be treated without respect is to be harmed. Therefore, P expects to be harmed by O and hence, according to Definition 5.5.5, cannot trust O. It follows that if P trusts O, then P believes that O respects P, which proves the theorem.

Note 5.5.8 Although respect has been proved to be a necessary condition of trust, it is not included in the list of basic preconditions because it may be derived from caring and understanding.

Theorem 5.5.9 *If P cares for O and P understands O, then P treats O with respect.*   Proof: According to Theorem 5.1.14, every person wants to be treated with respect. Hence, not to be treated with respect is to be harmed. But, it follows from Definition 5.2.1 that caring implies wanting not to harm, and it follows from Axioms 5.3.1 and 5.3.3 that understanding implies knowing what constitutes harm. It follows that, if P does not treat O with respect and hence, harms O, then either P does not care for O or P does not understand O, or both. From this the theorem follows.

Theorem 5.5.10 *If P trusts O, then P believes that O cares for P.*
Proof: If P believes that O does *not* care for P, then P must believe that O is indifferent to P and/or that O wants to harm P. (i) because, according to Axiom 5.5.2, P believes that O can harm P, and if P thinks that O is indifferent to P, then P believes that O may (happen to) harm P. From this it follows, according to the definition of trust (5.5.5), that P cannot trust O. (ii) If P believes that O can harm P (Axiom 5.5.2), and if P believes that O wants to harm P, then P believes that O may harm P. But, if P believes that O may harm P, then according to Definition 5.5.5, P cannot trust O. From (i) and (ii) the theorem follows.

Theorem 5.5.11 *If P trusts O, then P believes that O understands P.*
Proof: If P believes that O does not understand P, then P believes that O may harm P unintentionally, through misunderstanding. But, according to Definition 5.5.5, this means that P cannot trust O. By this the theorem is proved.

Note 5.5.12 Caring for someone implies interest in how one can benefit that person, and this makes it important to understand the person.

Theorem 5.5.13 *If P cares for O, then P wants to understand O.*
Proof: If P cares for O, then according to Definition 5.2.1, P wants O to feel good. But, according to Axiom 4.1.1 (O's feeling follows from O's awareness of the relationship between O's wants and O's beliefs), what makes O feel good follows from what O believes and wants. If this is a valid proposition, it follows from Axiom 3.7.15, that it is also a valid proposition that P believes that what makes O feel good follows from what O believes and wants. Because P wants to know how to make O feel good, it follows that P wants to know what O believes and wants. Hence, P must want to understand O, and by this the theorem is proved.

Note 5.5.14 The reason why understanding a person (knowing what a person believes and wants) must, nevertheless, be regarded as a separate condition of trust is that even though caring implies want to understand, it does not guarantee actual understanding. Persons who care for others may misunderstand and thereby, unintentionally harm them.
Note 5.5.15 Two factors relevant for trust have to do with the amount of *control* the other person is seen to have. If you believe that a person cannot control his or her own actions, then you cannot trust that person. The concept of *control* and one of its subcategories relevant here have already been defined, namely (5.4.0): "*P controls E*" = df "*P can make E occur and not occur according to P's wants,*" and (5.4.6): "*P has own-control of A*" = df "*P does or does not do A according to P's wants and independently of the wants of other persons.*" In addition, the concept of self-control, to be further treated in chapter 6, is relevant here:

Definition 6.4.1 *"P has self-control regarding act A"* = df *"P does or does not do A according to P's reflective wants and beliefs, and independently of P's unreflective wants and beliefs."*

Note 5.5.16 The numbering of the preceding proposition is determined by its topical belonging (in chapter 6) and not by its first occurrence in the text at this place.

Note 5.5.17 Lack of own-control can be observed, for example, when P is under pressure from parents, spouse, creditors, employer, and so on. Under such conditions, P may not be trustworthy. For example, P has promised to visit O but breaks that promise because P is forced by an employer to work overtime. O's trust in P may be weakened by this.

Lack of self-control can be found, for example, when a person is addicted to alcohol, narcotics, adultery, lying, stealing, or physical violence. Persons with such addictions are not trustworthy. You have self-control when you, unreflectively, want a drink and, reflectively, want not to want the drink, and when, as a consequence, you don't have the drink.

Note 5.5.18 To the extent that a person is thought to be lacking in own-control and/or self-control, he or she is not expected to act consistently and hence, cannot be trusted.

Theorem 5.5.19 *If P trusts O, then P believes that O has own-control*
Proof: If P believes that O does not have own-control (Definition 5.4.6), then P believes that O may be forced by others to harm P. Therefore, P cannot trust O. From this the theorem follows.

Theorem 5.5.20 *If P trusts O, then P believes that O has self-control.*
Proof: If P believes that O does not have self-control (Definition 6.4.1), then P believes that O may act towards P on the basis of unreflective wants and beliefs and, hence, may harm P. Therefore, P cannot trust O. From this the theorem follows.

Note 5.5.21 The preceding indicates that caring, understanding, own-control, and self-control each are necessary and irreducible conditions for trust. Respect is also necessary, but is derivable from caring and understanding. Are these four factors, taken together, sufficient to create trust? I think not. Even when they are fulfilled, one cannot trust a person if one does not believe that he or she is capable of coping with problems. One more condition needs to be added, namely *know-how*.

Theorem 5.5.22 *If P trusts O, then P believes that O has the relevant know-how.* Proof: If P does not believe that O has the relevant know-how, then P believes that O may be unable to avoid harming P or protecting P from harm. Hence, P cannot trust O. From this the theorem follows.

Note 5.5.23 The term "know-how" refers to what a person *can* do, that is, what it is possible for the person to do. It is not sufficient that you believe that your lawyer wants to benefit you, understands you, and has own-control and self-control. In order to trust your lawyer, you must also think that he or she has the relevant legal and other skills and knowledge. Obviously, power also enters into this category. What *can* be done may depend on the person's financial, military, political, or personal clout.

Note 5.5.24 The question remains of whether the five necessary conditions, when taken together, are sufficient to ensure trust?

Theorem 5.5.25 *P trusts O, if, and only if, P believes that O cares for P, O understands P, O has own-control, O has self-control, and O has the relevant know-how.* Proof of necessity: It has already been proved that each of the five conditions is necessary for trust to occur. Hence, their conjunction is also necessary. Proof of sufficiency: If O cares for P, that is, according to Definition 5.2.1, O wants P to feel good, and O believes that O can make P feel good, then it follows from Corollary 2.4.12 that O *tries* to make P feel good (see * below). From O having own-control and self-control, and O understanding P, it follows that O *can* protect P from harm originating in O. From O having the relevant know-how it follows that O *can* protect P from harm originating elsewhere. But, because harm must either originate in O or elsewhere, it follows that O can protect P from harm. If O tries to and can protect P from harm, it follows by Axiom 2.2.3 that O does protect P from harm. But if the preceding are taken to be consensually evident psychological propositions, it follows from Axiom 3.7.12 that P also believes in them and consequently, believes that O can protect P from harm. Hence, according to Definition 5.5.5, P trusts O. Therefore, the given conditions are sufficient for trust to occur. Because the given conditions have also been shown to be necessary, the theorem is proved.

* Corollary 2.4.12 requires that an act has the highest momentary expected utility in order to be tried out. This may be assured by assuming that the want to care for P is O's strongest momentary want, and that O is certain that O can make P feel good. These assumptions mean that the product of the want to benefit and the subjective likelihood of succeeding yield the highest momentary expected utility.

Note 5.5.26 The preceding indicates the necessary and sufficient conditions for trusting a person. It remains to inquire into the implications of trusting a person for the way one *acts*.

Theorem 5.5.27 *If P trusts O, then P believes that O will try to protect P from harm.* Proof: If P does not believe that O will try to protect P from harm, then P believes that O may harm P by not protecting P. From this it follows by Definition 5.5.5, that P cannot trust O. This proves the theorem.

Corollary 5.5.28 *If P's trust in O decreases, then P's expectancy of being harmed by O increases.* Proof: The corollary follows directly from Definition 5.5.5.

Theorem 5.5.29 *If P's trust in O decreases, then P's tolerance of ambiguity in matters having to do with O decreases also.*   Proof: According to 5.5.28 if P's trust in O decreases, then P's expectancy of being harmed by O increases. But, if P's expectancy of being harmed by O increases, and P wants to be prepared for that increasing danger, then it becomes increasingly important for P to know whether or not, and in what way, the danger is imminent. This means that P's want to resolve relevant ambiguity (Theorem 3.6.7) increases, that is, P becomes less tolerant of ambiguity. Hence the theorem is proved.

Theorem 5.5.30 *If P's trust in O decreases, then P will treat O more guardedly.*   Proof: If P's trust in O decreases, then according to Corollary 5.5.28, P's expectancy of being harmed by O increases. If to treat someone "guardedly" means to act in anticipation of being harmed, then the theorem follows directly.

Note 5.5.31 In summary, a number of wants and beliefs are shared by all persons. These include the want to be treated with *respect* and to behave *respectably* toward others, the want to be *cared* for and to *care* for someone, the want to be *understood* by others and to *understand* them, and the want to have *own-control* and *self-control*.

The joint outcome of various combinations of the preceding variables are varying degrees of unilateral or mutual *trust*. A number of propositions are given, relating trust to antecedent and consequent conditions.

Chapter 6

Intrapersonal Processes

Note 6.0.0 Reflectivity is the foundation for what may be called the intrapsychic domain. Being aware THAT one is aware of something, means that the awareness as such, and the bearer of this awareness, come into existence *for* the individual. Reflectivity is involved in all intrapersonal processes, as the term is used here. Examples: P is aware that P is aware of X, P believes Y about P's belief X, P wants P to want X, and P feels Y about P's feeling Z about X. The last case may be exemplified by, P is angry at P because P is afraid to do A.

Note 6.0.1 In ordinary language there is a striking parallel between interpersonal and intrapersonal processes. Respect, care, understanding, control, and trust relating to other persons have their counterparts in self-respect, self-care, self-understanding, self-control, and self-trust. Every interpersonal proposition involving two persons, P and O, can be transformed into an intrapersonal proposition, by substituting a term P for the term O. The outcome are formulae with two P's.

Note 6.0.2 The transformation from interpersonal to intrapersonal is reversible. Hence, every proposition involving two P's can be transformed into an interpersonal proposition by substituting the term O for one of the P's.

Note 6.0.3 The doubling of P in intrapersonal propositions represents the *reflectivity* of mental processes. P is both the reflective agent and the target of the reflection, that is, P exists *for* P. Language allows not only for reflective beliefs, but also for reflective wants, as in "P wants P not to want X." A consequence of introducing both reflective beliefs and reflective wants is that one can also talk about reflective feelings of the type "P is angry with P for being afraid of A." Finally, there are actions directed at self, an extreme variant of which is *suicide*.

Note 6.0.4 When a person is asked to describe him or herself, reflectivity is directly involved. P is a describer of P and P is described by P. There is no sharp distinction between the two Ps. For example, P may comment on her own self-description, saying "it's typical of me to use so many words in describing myself." The "me" in this sentence refers both to the describer of P and the described person P. The person making the description and the person described are fused.

Note 6.0.5 In what follows, the intrapsychic counterparts of the interpersonal factors *respect*, *care*, *understanding*, *control*, and *trust*, are treated. The interpersonal propositions dealing with the above five variables, introduced in chapter 5, are transformed into intrapersonal propositions and their validity is examined. At stake is the following very general axiom (P*O = any psychological proposition,involving P and O):

Axiom 6.0.6 *P*O is a consensually self-evident interpersonal proposition, if, and only if, P*P is a consensually self-evident intrapersonal proposition.*

Corollary 6.0.7 *If P*O is consensually self-evident, then P*P is consensually self-evident.* Proof: This follows directly from Axiom 6.0.6.

Corollary 6.0.8 *If P*P is consensually self-evident, then P*O is consensually self-evident.* Proof: This follows directly from Axiom 6.0.6.

Note 6.0.9 Suppose that "P can surprise O only by presenting O with something unexpected" is a consensually self-evident proposition. Then, it follows from 6.0.6 that "P can surprise P only by presenting P with something unexpected" is also consensually self-evident. It is, however, hard to find examples of this latter proposition, since the two P's tend to have access to the same information.

Note 6.0.10 In what follows, the intrapersonal equivalents of the interpersonal propositions of chapter 5 are presented.

6.1 Self-Respect

Definition 6.1.0 *"P respects P"* = df *"P regards P as someone who ought to be treated rightly."*

Definition 6.1.1 *"P treats P with respect"* = df *"P treats P rightly."*

Note 6.1.2 Definitions 6.1.0 and 6.1.1 correspond to Definitions 5.1.1 and 5.1.2 in the interpersonal domain. However, P treats P with respect, cannot mean that P acts toward P in respectful ways, but means that P acts respectably, that is, in such a way that P's duties are fulfilled. Hence, P can be proud of P. If P acts disrespectfully, P can be ashamed of P, be angry with P, and so on. In ordinary language, it is meaningful to say that a person tries to act in a way that maintains his or her self-respect.

Note 6.1.3 Definition 6.1.0 refers to the *attitude* of self-respect, whereas Definition 6.1.1 refers to the *expression* of this attitude. Self-respect must be distinguished from *self-admiration* and *self-awe* (cf. Note 5.1.13).

Theorem 6.1.4 *P wants to be treated with respect by P and wants to behave respectably.* Proof: Analogous to that of Theorem 5.1.14.

Note 6.1.5 The two parts of Theorem 6.1.4 are intimately connected. A person can only treat him or herself with respect by behaving respectably.

Theorem 6.1.6 *If P respects P, then P wants to treat P with respect.*
Proof: Analogous to that of Theorem 5.1.6.

Corollary 6.1.7 *P tries to treat P with respect, if, and only if, treating P with respect has the highest expected utility for P.*   Proof: Analogous to that of Corollary 5.1.10.

Corollary 6.1.8 *If treating P with respect has the highest expected utility for P, and if P can treat P with respect, then P will treat P with respect.*
Proof: This follows from Corollary 6.1.7 and Axiom 2.2.3 (P does A, if, and only if, P can do A, and P tries to do A).

Note 6.1.9 The particular use of the two preceding corollaries is, again, to emphasize that behaving respectably interpersonally, is reinforced by an intrapersonal component. I try to behave respectably not only because, otherwise, I hurt others, but also because, otherwise, I hurt myself.

Corollary 6.1.10 *If P treats P without respect, then P treats P wrongly.*
Proof: Analogous to that of Corollary 5.1.3.

Note 6.1.11 Corollary 6.1.10 states that behaving nonrespectably means doing wrong against oneself. One ought not to do this, and it leads to numerous negative consequences, both internal and external. Hence, an offender may say "I have merely hurt *myself*," or "*I* am the one who will suffer most," or "How can I have done this to myself?"

Note 6.1.12 There are two main conditions under which a person's self-respect is lowered. One is when a person is not treated with respect by others, and the other is when a person is not behaving respectably, that is, is not treated with respect by him or herself. If a child is not treated with respect, self-respect cannot develop. Depending on the seriousness of this condition, the individual may come to regard him or herself as being more or less without rights and duties.

If an adult is, intentionally, treated without respect, the normal response is *anger*. If the absence of respect is consistent and prolonged, and if anger leads nowhere, the outcome may be *despair* and *depression* (cf. the treatment of feeling in chapter 4).

If a person for some reason begins and continues to behave nonrespectably, the person may cope with this either by ceasing to accept the norms involved (becoming an outlaw, antisocial, or asocial), which involves finding other reference groups with other norms, or by trying to escape the self-loathing by avoiding relevant topics as much as possible. "I do not want to talk about this," or "I do not want to hear one word about that," or "don't remind me of it," and so on.

6.2 *Self-Care*

Definition 6.2.0 "*P cares for P*" = df "*P wants P to feel good.*"

Theorem 6.2.1 *If P cares for P, then P feels good when P feels good.*
Proof: Analogous to the proof of Theorem 5.2.5.

Theorem 6.2.2 *If P cares for P, then P feels bad when P feels bad.*
Proof: Analogous to the proof of Theorem 5.2.6.

Note 6.2.3 In the two preceding theorems, the two P's feel differently. In Theorem 6.2.1, P unreflectively feels good about something, and P reflectively feels good because P is feeling good. In Theorem 6.2.2, P, unreflectively, feels bad about something, and P, reflectively, feels bad about P feeling bad. The two sources of P's feeling good and P's feeling bad are, respectively, unreflective and reflective. The unreflective feeling about something is reinforced by the reflective feeling about the unreflective one. The two theorems indicate that reflection intensifies feelings when self-care is involved. This makes sense, and is expressed in common advice such as "try not to think about your pain" (ignore it, think about something else). The implicit premise here is that thinking about, that is, reflecting on the pain, intensifies it.

Theorem 6.2.4 *If P cares for P, then P wants to keep track of how things go with P.*   Proof: Analogous to the proof of Theorem 5.2.3.

Note 6.2.5 P is in an optimal position for keeping track of what is going on with respect to P, and, normally does so. However, there appear to be occasions in which self-care is weaker than other wants P may have. Other persons may have to remind P to eat enough, to get some sleep, to do something about a persistent illness, and so on. Some people appear to be truly indifferent to, or even take malicious pleasure in, their own suffering. That self-care is variable is also reflected, for example, in phrases such as "take care of yourself!"
Note 6.2.6 The intensifying effect of reflection is known in clinical work, for example in the case of *fear* or *depression*. The primary experience of fear in a given situation is made much worse by the secondary or reflective fear, the *fear of fear.* Similarly, the primary feeling of depression is made worse by the reflective depression. "I get so depressed by being depressed." Frequently, the reflective emotion is not identical to the primary one. A person may, for example, be afraid of being angry or be angry about being afraid.

Theorem 6.2.7 *If P cares for P, then P tries to make P feel good, unless other acts have a higher expected utility for P.*   Proof: Analogous to the proof of Theorem 5.2.4.

Note 6.2.8 The distinction between caring and liking in the interpersonal domain (Definitions 5.2.1 and 5.2.7) also applies to the intrapersonal domain. However, lack of caring for and disliking of self are more rare and dramatic than lack of caring for and disliking of other persons.

Definition 6.2.9 *"P likes P"* = df *"P feels good being with P."*

Note 6.2.10 Everyday language contains sentences such as "I dislike myself," or "I am fed up with myself," or "I am not a sympathetic person." P is forced to be with him or herself, except in situations where he or she becomes "unself-conscious." This may happen in work, when being entertained, and in some social situations. P can also get rid of P, temporarily, by using alcohol or drugs, or by going to sleep, and, permanently, by committing suicide.

Note 6.2.11 Some persons complain that they are compulsively self-reflective, that they cannot do anything without observing themselves. This condition is particularly painful, when the reflective observer is harshly critical and condemning.

Axiom 6.2.12 *P wants to care for P.*

Note 6.2.13 This axiom is stronger than the corresponding interpersonal Axiom 5.2.10 (every person wants to care for someone) because it asserts that a person *always* wants to care for him or herself. In everyday life, a person may say, "I want to pamper myself," or "I will treat myself to a nice dinner and an evening in the opera." However, Axiom 6.2.12 says nothing about the relative strength of the want to care for oneself. Hence, it does not exclude cases where other wants are stronger, and where the person risks his or her welfare or even life.

Theorem 6.2.14 *P wants to be cared for by P.* Proof: Analogous to that of Theorem 5.2.12.

Note 6.2.15 Axiom 6.2.12 and Theorem 6.2.14 taken together indicate a double positive feeling involved in self-care. One feels good both in taking care of oneself and in being taken care of by oneself.

6.3 *Self-Understanding*

Note 6.3.0 Understanding has already been introduced as a primitive term (5.3.0). The necessary and sufficient conditions of self-understanding may be derived from the corresponding interpersonal axioms.

Corollary 6.3.1 *"P understands what P means by saying or doing A, to the extent that P agrees with P as to what, for P, is equivalent to A, implied by A, contradicted by A, and irrelevant to A."* Proof: This follows directly from Axiom 5.3.1, by substituting P for O.

Corollary 6.3.2 *P understands why P does A, if, and only if, P agrees with P about which wants and beliefs of P are involved in P doing A.*   P r o o f : This follows directly from Axiom 5.3.3, by substituting P for O.

Note 6.3.3 At first sight, the extrapolations from the interpersonal to the intrapersonal domain in Corollaries 6.3.1 and 6.3.2 may appear implausible and artificial. Normally, one takes it for granted that one understands what one is saying and doing and why. However, this is also true to a large extent about understanding what another person is saying and doing and why. Hence, it may be that the difference is one of degree only. In both cases, there are large areas of understanding which are superficial but veridical. Example: P says to O, "pass me the butter please!" Presumably both P and O understand fully what P means by this statement. In other words, there is consensus with respect to the criteria of Corollaries 6.3.1 and 6.3.2.

It is also easy to find examples of when O does not fully understand what P is saying or why P is saying it. It remains to consider possible examples where P does not fully understand what P is saying or doing, and why. Consider the following examples, not infrequently heard in everyday life: "I have only now realized what my acting means," "Now, I finally understand what I wanted to say, when I said that," "I don't understand why I said that," "I don't understand why I am doing this."

Theorem 6.3.4 *P wants to be understood by P and wants to understand P.* Proof: Analogous to proof of Theorem 5.3.7.

Note 6.3.5 The two wants in Theorem 6.3.4 interact. The want to be understood and the want to understand combine to yield an intensified resultant want. This may be expressed in the following theorem:

Theorem 6.3.6 *Other things equal, P's want to understand P is stronger than P's want to understand O, and P's want to be understood by P is stronger than P's want to be understood by O.*   Proof: Suppose that, other things equal, P's want to understand P and P's want to understand O are equally strong. But, because the goal of P's want to understand P is identical to the goal of P's want to be understood by P, and they both are wants of P, they are compatible, and it follows from Theorem 3.3.17 that they sum to a want stronger than P's want to understand P alone. The latter want is assumed to be equal to P's want to understand O. But, P's want to understand O and P's want to be understood by O have different goals and, hence, do not summate to one want. It follows that P's combined want to understand and to be understood by P, must be stronger than P's want to understand O and P's want to be understood by O.

6.4 Self-Control

Note 6.4.0 This concept is widely used, and evidently refers to important mental phenomena. Its interpersonal analogues are *own-control* (Definition 5.4.6) and *other-control* (Definition 5.4.8). Self-control may be defined as follows:

> Definition 6.4.1 *"P has self-control regarding act A"* = df *"P does or does not do A according to P's reflective wants and beliefs, and independently of P's unreflective wants and beliefs."*

Note 6.4.2 According to Definition 6.4.1, lack of self-control means that when P's reflective and unreflective wants and beliefs are in conflict, P acts according to the unreflective ones. How can lack of self-control be understood in terms of the present system? It represents a deviation from the normal state of integration formulated in Axiom 1.2.16, and involves the performance of acts that the person reflectively regards as wrong. Lack of self-control presupposes the presence of reflective awareness (Definition 1.4.2). According to Axiom 1.4.11 this means that the person can *talk about* the lack of self-control, that is, the fact that he or she does something he or she does not reflectively want to do, and does not do what he or she reflectively wants to do. It follows from Corollary 2.4.12 that, for the person acting without self-control, the unreflective act momentarily has a higher expected utility than the reflective act. This means that the person must be acting according to other wants and beliefs than those reflectively regarded as the correct ones. In other words, the *context* of acting, that is, what is taken into account in acting (Definition 1.2.19), must be different. It is common knowledge that when there is lack of self-control, the person's context for acting is temporally *narrower* than that involved in the person's reflective awareness. The person is a victim of the here-and-now, his or her momentary impressions, temptations, and impulses. What is known about long term consequences is not taken into account. Among such consequences is being held responsible for one's actions (Axiom 1.3.4) and hence, the person's actions without self-control can be described as irresponsible.

Note 6.4.3 The preceding means that there is a reflective, responsible level in a person and also an unreflective, irresponsible one. Reflectivity implies awareness of time and context and consideration of possible alternatives to, and long term consequences of, every act. Unreflectivity means responding automatically to the immediately given. Lack of self-control means animal-like behavior.

Note 6.4.4 Persons with high self-control are said to function well. This means that they act according to what they reflectively regard as right. However, high self-control should not be confused with compulsive restraint of all spontaneity. High self-control is compatible with a high degree of spontaneity in situations judged to be appropriate for this, in the context of the total life situation. Hence, high self-control involves maximal flexibility. Compulsivity is a sign of *low* self-control. The compulsive person *cannot* let go, that is, act in the here-and-now, even when he or she regards this as the right thing to do. Compulsivity involves automatic, unreflective control. It should be noted that there is no paradox of the type "be spontaneous" involved here. One can reflectively decide to *relinquish* control. This is setting aside a fenced-in area for play, where only the perimeter is reflectively monitored.

6.5 Self-Trust

Note 6.5.0 The analogous conceptualization of the inter- and intrapersonal domains also extends to the concept of trust. P feels vulnerable not only in relation to O, but also in relation to P. Hence the following axiom of self-vulnerability can be formulated:

Axiom 6.5.1 *P believes that P can harm P.*

Definition 6.5.2 "*P trusts P*" = df "*P believes P will not do anything bad to P.*" This is what is meant by self-trust.

Note 6.5.3 In what follows, the necessary and sufficient conditions of self-trust are listed, in complete analogy to the corresponding conditions of trust of others.

Theorem 6.5.4 *If P trusts P, then P believes that P respects P.*   P r o o f : Analogous to the proof of Theorem 5.5.7.

Theorem 6.5.5 *If P cares for P and P understands P, then P treats P with respect.*   Proof: Analogous to the proof of Theorem 5.5.9.

Theorem 6.5.6 *If P trusts P, then P believes that P cares for P.*   P r o o f : Analogous to the proof of Theorem 5.5.10.

Theorem 6.5.7 *If P trusts P, then P believes that P understands P* Proof: Identical to the proof of Theorem 5.5.11.

Theorem 6.5.8 *If P cares for P, then P wants to understand P.*   Proof: Analogous to the proof of Theorem 5.5.13.

Theorem 6.5.9 *If P trusts P, then P believes that P has own control.* Proof: Analogous to the proof of Theorem 5.5.19.

Theorem 6.5.10 *If P trusts P, then P believes that P has self-control.* Proof: Analogous to the proof of Theorem 5.5.20.

Theorem 6.5.11 *If P trusts P, then P believes that P has the relevant know-how.*   Proof: Identical to the proof of Theorem 5.5.22.

Theorem 6.5.12 *P trusts P, if, and only if, P believes that P cares for P, P understands P, P has own-control, P has self-control, and P has the relevant know-how.* Proof: Analogous to the proof of Theorem 5.5.25.

Note 6.5.13 The complete analogy between the interpersonal and the intrapersonal as far as conditions of trust are concerned is equally compelling when it comes to the implications of trust.

Theorem 6.5.14 *If P trusts P, then P believes that P will try to protect P from harm.* Proof: Analogous to the proof of theorem 5.5.27.

Corollary 6.5.15 *If P's trust in P decreases, then P's expectancy of being harmed by P increases.* Proof: Analogous to the proof of Corollary 5.5.28.

Theorem 6.5.16 *If P's trust in P decreases, then P's tolerance of ambiguity in matters having to do with P decreases too.* Proof: Analogous to the proof of Theorem 5.5.29.

Theorem 6.5.17 *If P's trust in P decreases, then P will treat P more guardedly.* Proof: Analogous to the proof of Theorem 5.5.30.

Note 6.5.19 The interpersonal variables, respect, care, understanding, own-control, and perceived know-how of the other one, all have their intrapersonal analogues: self-respect, self-care, self-understanding, self-control, and perceived know-how of oneself. The same necessary and sufficient factors (care, understanding, own-control, self-control, and know-how) determine trust in others and trust in self.

Chapter 7

Personal Change

Note 7.0.0 Changes in personal activity occur all the time. Each change is, in principle, ambiguous in that it may reflect either a change in the dispositions of the person, or a change in the external or internal circumstances influencing the person. When a former scoundrel starts behaving respectably, the question is always, has he or she changed for the better, or is it merely an adjustment to new external circumstances. One may distinguish between *first-order* and *second-order* changes.

7.1. *Types of Change*

Definition 7.1.0. *"First-order change"* = df *"A change that reflects variations in external and/or internal conditions."*

Note 7.1.1 First order changes are strictly reversible. Given the question "What day is it today?" P answers "Tuesday," and, when asked the identical question the next day, answers "Wednesday." This variation in acting is a reversible first-order change, which does not indicate any change in the dispositions of the person, but only in the external circumstances. One week later, the person again answers "Tuesday." Another example: Given the question "Are you hungry?" P answers "Yes." P then has dinner, and on being given the same question, now answers "No." This change too is strictly reversible, and does not indicate that the person has changed. When asked the same question five hours later, the person again answers "Yes." Some first-order changes, although themselves reversible, reflect irreversible changes in external or internal conditions. Given the question "Has the train left?" the person answers "No." A little later, and from then on, the person answers "Yes" to the same question. Similarly, given the question "Do you read without glasses?" the person answers "Yes," but, some years later, and from then on, answers "No" to the same question. However, first-order changes are never irreversible in themselves, but always reflect changes in the circumstances surrounding the person, including the person's body. In principle, they can be reversed, if the external circumstances are reversed. If it turns out that the last train has not left after all, or if the person, after an operation, regains his or her ability to read without glasses, the answers of the person will be correspondingly reversed. First-order changes are part of the process of keeping track of and adjusting to the actual situation.

Definition 7.1.2 *"Second-order change"* = df *"A change in disposition given constant internal and external conditions"* .

Note 7.1.3 Second-order changes are strictly irreversible. They consist of outcomes of learning from experience (Axiom 1.5.2) and involve changes of the person. The test for the occurrence of such learning is to observe whether or not the person's activity has changed, given constant external and internal conditions. Learning a language, becoming able to drive a car, getting to know a person, are examples of second-order variations.

Note 7.1.4 The following example is intended to illustrate how a second-order change can be a change in the repeated pattern of first-order changes. A rebellious young person has for some time tried always to cross streets on the red light and to wait on the green light. This is a stable pattern of first-order changes; change to red light instigates walking, change to green light instigates stopping. In the process of coming of age, the person changes to become a law-abiding citizen. From now on, he or she stops on the red light and crosses on the green. A new pattern of first-order changes has emerged, and this appears to constitute a second-order change. However, actual cases of change always involve an element of uncertainty. Suppose that all the street light sequences occur in a film studio and that the young person is played by an actor according to a script. In this case, the actor is not undergoing a second-order change, but is merely displaying first-order changes. This becomes particularly clear when the director is dissatisfied, and the scenes have to be retaken.

Note 7.1.5 A defining difference between first- and second- order changes is that the former are always reversible, whereas the latter are always irreversible. This distinction has already been discussed in chapter 1. First-order changes are incorporated into reversible systems involving principles of conservation, whereas second-order changes involve irreversible modifications of the person's dispositional structure.

Note 7.1.6 The basic types of dispositions organizing a person's activity involve either *knowledge* or *preference*. Knowledge manifested in awareness is called *belief* (know-that), and knowledge manifested in the way acts are carried out is called *skill* (know-how). Preference manifested in awareness is called *want* and preference manifested in how acts are carried out is called *style* (preferred ways of acting). An act always involves belief, skill, want, and style. In order to isolate these factors as determinants of choice, one needs a situation that allows for two, and only two, alternative acts. A choice of one of them indicates relative strength of *belief*, if the contents of the expected outcomes are identical, if the expected exertion is identical, if the acts can only be performed in one way, and if only the likelihoods of attaining the goal differ. This likelihood can be divided into two components, namely the likelihood that the person can successfully perform the act, and the likelihood that the act leads to the goal. A choice indicates relative strength of *want*, if the likelihoods of achieving the goal are equal, if the expected exertion is equal, if the acts can only be performed in one way, and if only the attractiveness of the expected goals varies. A choice indicates differences in preferred *style*, if the likelihoods of achieving the goal are equal, if the expected exertion is equal, if the attractiveness of the goals is equal, and if only the way in which the acts can be performed varies. Finally, a choice indicates laziness (want to avoid exertion), if the likelihoods of achieving the goals are equal, if the attractiveness of the goals is equal, if the acts can only be performed in one way, and if only the expected exertion varies.

Note 7.1.7 The preceding may be summarized as follows: Isolated changes in acting are ambiguous. They may be adjustments to changes in the momentary situation (first-order) or changes in dispositions (second-order). First-order changes are reversible and second-order changes are irreversible. Dispositions are of four kinds, *beliefs (know-that), skills (know-how), wants (preferences in goals), style (preferences in performance)*.

7.2. Open and Closed Systems of Dispositions

Note 7.2.0 Personal processes may involve *open* or *closed* systems of dispositions. A closed system is characterized by allowing only first-order, reversible changes. It rejects information it cannot incorporate, and cannot be changed by any counterevidence. If the system includes the dispositional belief "if X then Y," and "X and not-Y" is observed, then this is taken to be evidence, not that "if X then Y" is wrong, but that the observation must be wrong. Similarly, if the dispositional skill is such that problems of type X must be solved by procedures of type x, and an instance of X does not respond to a procedure of type x, this is not taken to invalidate the system, but is merely taken as evidence that, either the problem is not really of type X or the procedure is not really of type x. Next, if the dispositional want is to have X and having X does not result in the expected pleasure, this is taken to mean that either it was not really X that was achieved, or that there really was pleasure, albeit masked by other experiences or states. Finally, if the dispositional style involves preference for doing something in the manner x, and if doing it in the manner x does not feel right, this is taken to indicate that either it was not really done in the manner x, or it really felt right, but that the feeling was masked by other irrelevant experiences or states.

Note 7.2.1 A classical, intensely studied, example of a closed system is the concept of *conservation*. If a person has achieved such a concept, and is then shown an apparent falsification (two equally heavy balls of plasticine, one ball deformed into a sausage, ball now appears to be heavier than sausage, as indicated on a pair of scales) the concept is, typically, not given up. Instead the person will argue that something is the matter, mechanically, with the scales, that something has been lost on the floor, or has stuck to the hand, that the experimenter has cheated, and so on. The concept of *conservation*, in so far as it is taken to be self-evident, is not at stake.

Similar closed systems can be found in people's views of moral, political, religious, and other matters. A person's conception of self and of intimate others, is, typically, a closed system that can incorporate almost any event without changing. In psychotherapy, the task is often to try to open up closed and maladaptive systems.

Note 7.2.2 Open systems are, in principle, sensitive to experience and argument and hence, admit second order change. Three theorems are central in this connection:

Theorem 7.2.3 *If P is aware of and takes it to be relevant that X is sometimes followed by Y and sometimes followed by Z, and that both Y and Z occur only after X, then P will want to find subcategories of X, Xy and Xz, such that Xy is always followed by Y and Xz is always followed by Z.*

Proof: Without having found subcategories of the mentioned type, P's belief about what will follow after X will often be erroneous. Because, according to Axiom 3.6.2, P wants to believe what is the case, it follows that P will want to find subcategories of X that make correct prediction possible.

Note 7.2.4 Theorem 7.2.3 describes a search for *relevant differentiating cues.* Whether or not a person will actually search for such cues in a given situation at a given time, obviously depends on the relative strength of other wants active at that time, and on what activity has the highest momentary expected utility.

Theorem 7.2.5 *If P is aware of and takes it to be relevant that X is always followed by Z and Y is always followed by Z, and Z occurs only after X or Y, then P will want to find and try out indices of type b, common to X and Y, such that b is always followed by Z and -b is always followed by not-Z.*

Proof: Because having two hypotheses and two explanations involves more exertion than having only one hypothesis and one explanation, and because P wants to minimize exertion (Axiom 2.4.7), it follows that P will want to find ways to simplify the prediction and explanation of Z.

Note 7.2.6 It is taken for granted that prediction from or to a disjunctive concept involves more cognitive effort than prediction to or from a conjunctive concept. Theorem 7.2.5 describes a want to find a *relevant common factor.* Whether or not a person will actually search for such a factor in a given situation at a given time depends on the relative strength of the other wants active at that time, and on what activity has the highest expected utility.

Theorem 7.2.7 *If P is aware of and takes it to be relevant that a member of category X is followed by a member of category Y, and no other information, taken by P to be relevant, is available, then P will tentatively believe that a new member of X will be followed by a new member of Y.* Proof: According to Axiom 1.5.15, P's awareness of the future consists of extrapolations from P's awareness of trends in the past. P is aware of a trend in the past where an X is followed by a Y. Because no other information is assumed to be available to

P, it follows from Axiom 1.5.15 that P will expect another X to be followed by another Y.

Note 7.2.8 Theorem 7.2.7 describes what may be labeled the principle that equals are expected to be followed by equals. This is another basic psychological principle.

Note 7.2.9 Given that there exists a set X and a set Y such that a member of X is always followed by a member of Y, and given that P searches for such a combination of sets, the probability that P will find it is dependent on the probability that P will notice that an X is actually followed by a Y. In practice, one always tries to optimalize the conditions for learning through increasing the *salience* of the relevant events. The term "salience" refers to the likelihood that something will be recognized. The perceptual conditions of recognition include such factors as size, intensity, movement against a stationary background, and, most efficient, the direct pointing out or mentioning of the relevant events or features. It should be added, however, that the mere sequencing of salient events does not necessarily lead to an expectancy that there is a regularity. Such expectancies are profoundly influenced by the person's already existing conception of the world, or in the case of infants, by their genetically determined predispositions. Note the highly variable difficulties in conditioning responses to different kinds of stimuli. From everyday adult life, one example should suffice. A person spills coffee on the floor and immediately after that, the siren of an ambulance is heard. Both events are very salient and the person is clearly aware of them. Nevertheless, no expectancy is formed that spilling coffee on the floor will be followed by the sound of an ambulance. The reason is that this does not fit into the person's view of the causal structure of the world. In other words, too many and too extensive changes would have to be made in the structure of the subjective world to incorporate such a regularity. There is a reluctance to change that may be expressed in the following theorem.

Theorem 7.2.10 *A person's belief system will change in the least extensive way possible, taken by that person to eliminate a recognized inconsistency.* Proof: An inconsistency makes the situation ambiguous. It follows from Theorem 3.6.7 that a person wants to resolve relevant ambiguity. It also follows from Axiom 2.4.7 that a person wants to minimize exertion. Hence, a person selects the way of eliminating a recognized inconsistency that appears to involve the least exertion. From this, and the assumption that the least extensive change also requires the least exertion, the theorem follows.

Note 7.2.11 The problems that lead people to visit a psychologist usually involve unrealistic closed belief-want-systems linked with negative feelings and acts of low utility. A task of psychotherapy is to open up such systems up, so that they can change. How this is possible is an important theoretical as well as practical problem.

Note 7.2.12 The task of differentiating between first- and second-order change and between open and closed systems is often difficult. There are many changes that are hard to classify clearly as first- or second-order, and there are systems that are only relatively open or closed. At the one extreme, there are easily reversible momentary adjustments that do not involve changes in the person's dispositions. At the other extreme, there are discriminations and differentiations that change the person's repertory for ever, and can never be undone.

Note 7.2.13 Currently popular measures of therapeutic effect, such as changes in therapist's and client's responses to questionnaires and inventories, rarely allow for any clear distinction between first- and second-order change. Because they are susceptible to context effects of various kinds, their meaning is highly ambiguous. Only evidence that a person is now capable of making discriminations and differentiations that he or she *could not possibly* have made earlier, should be taken as certain evidence of second-order change. Other changes should most naturally be interpreted as first-order changes reflecting the changing relationship between client and therapist and the context of a more or less prolonged and perhaps, expensive interaction. The recorded changes may be well within the range of the client's pre-existing closed system repertory.

Note 7.2.14 Procedures aimed at enabling a person to change may be directed at abilities, wants, beliefs, feelings, or acts. However, because these are not conceptually unrelated, every procedure will tend to involve several or all of them. Because acting always involves all five categories, the conditions of change in acting are considered first. Later, procedures specifically directed at changing abilities, wants, beliefs, and feelings are described.

7.3 Changes in Acting

Note 7.3.0 The conditions for acting are expressed in Axiom 2.2.3 (P does A, if, and only if, P can do A, and P tries to do A). From this two corollaries about change may be derived.

Corollary 7.3.1. *P changes from doing A to not doing A, if, and only if, there is a change from P can do A to P cannot do A and/or a change from P tries to do A to P does not try to do A.* Proof: This follows directly from Axiom 2.2.3.

Corollary 7.3.2. *P changes from not doing A to doing A, if, and only if, there is a change from P cannot do A to P can do A and/or a change from P does not try to do A to P tries to do A.* Proof: This follows directly from Axiom 2.2.3.

Note 7.3.3 Axiom 1.5.15 (P's awareness of the future consists of extrapolations from P's awareness of trends in the past) implies that intentional activity, which is always oriented by beliefs about the future, can only change if one has new experiences and hence, becomes aware of new trends. The following corollary may be derived (see Theorem 26, Smedslund, 1982c).

Corollary 7.3.4 *If P does not try to do A, and if no other circumstances intervene, then P does not improve P's performance on A.*   Proof: This follows directly from Axiom 1.5.15.

Note 7.3.5 A change in acting in the same context always means either a change in can or a change in trying or a change in both can and trying. The next step is to formulate separately the conditions for a change in can (ability) and in trying.

7.4 Changes in Can (Ability)

Note 7.4.0 The conditions of can are expressed in Axiom 2.3.3 (P can do A, if and only if, P's ability to do A is greater than the difficulty of doing A). Three corollaries about change may be derived from this axiom.

Corollary 7.4.1 *There is a change from P can do A to P cannot do A, if, and only if, (a) P's ability to do A has decreased and/or (b) the difficulty for P of A has increased; the net effect of (a) and (b) being a change from P's ability to do A being greater than the difficulty of A for P, to P's ability to do A being smaller than the difficulty of A for P.*   Proof: This follows directly from Axiom 2.3.3.

Corollary 7.4.2 *There is a change from P cannot do A to P can do A, if, and only if, (a) P's ability to do A has increased and/or (b) the difficulty for P of A has decreased; the net effect of (a) and (b) being a change from P's ability to do A being lower than the difficulty for P of A, to P's ability to do A being higher than the difficulty for P of A.*   Proof: This follows directly from Axiom 2.3.3.

Corollary 7.4.3 *The effect of any increment or decrement in the ability of P to do A can be compensated by a corresponding increment or decrement in the difficulty for P of A and vice versa.*   Proof: This follows directly from Axiom 2.3.3.

Note 7.4.4 The preceding three corollaries, expressing the effect of changes in ability and difficulty on can, are routinely used in everyday life. The present system contains no principles for what determines changes in ability and difficulty. However, it is apparent that a detailed analysis of the components of specific abilities and difficulties will enable one to predict what learning and what situational changes will lead to required behavioral changes.

The next step is to formulate the effects of component variables on changes in trying.

7.5 Changes in Trying

Note 7.5.0 The conditions of trying are expressed in Corollary 2.4.13 (P tries to do A, if, and only if, A is the act which, for P, has the highest expected utility). From this corollary at least four other corollaries about the conditions of change in trying may be derived.

Corollary 7.5.1 *There is a change from P trying to do A, to P not trying to do A, if, and only if, the expected utility, for P, of trying to do A, changes from being the highest to not being the highest.* Proof: This follows directly from Corollary 2.4.13.

Corollary 7.5.2. *There is a change from P not trying to do A to P trying to do A, if, and only if, the expected utility, for P, of trying to do A changes from not being to being the highest.* Proof: This follows directly from Corollary 2.4.13.

Note 7.5.3. Because changes in expected utility can come about either through changes in strength of the relevant wants or in strength of the relevant beliefs, or in both, a couple of more specific corollaries may be derived from Corollary 2.4.13.

Corollary 7.5.4. *If there is a change from P trying to do A to P not trying to do A, then (a) P's want to do A has declined in strength relative to P's other wants, and/or (b) P's belief that trying to do A will succeed has declined in strength relative to P's other beliefs.* Proof: This follows directly from Definition 2.4.11 and Corollary 2.4.13.

Corollary 7.5.5 *If there is a change from P not trying to do A, to P trying to do A, then (a) P's want to do A has increased in strength relative to P's other wants, and/or (b) P's belief that trying to do A will succeed has increased in strength relative to P's other beliefs.* Proof: This follows directly from Definition 2.4.11 and Corollary 2.4.13.

Note 7.5.6 Although the main determinant of trying, expected utility, is the product of only two variables, namely strength of want and strength of belief, each of these is the result of two components. Strength of want is equal to the strength of the want to reach the goal, minus the strength of the want to avoid exertion. Hence, the strength of the want to try to reach a goal varies according to the degree of exertion required by the alternative means of reaching that goal. This analysis can also be applied to the interesting special case where the goal is precisely to exert oneself, for example, because it is believed to be healthy.

Similarly, the strength of the belief that trying to do a certain act will lead to the goal is the result of two components, namely the strength of the belief that the person can perform the act, and the strength of the belief that the act leads to the goal. Hence, the strength of the belief that trying to do the act will lead to the goal is the product of the strength of the belief that the person can successfully perform the act, and the strength of the belief that the act leads to the goal. These four factors are, in turn, the outcomes of certain antecedents and hence, yield a number of formal propositions involving changes in the determinants of trying, wants, and beliefs.

7.6 Changes in Strength of Wants

Note 7.6.0 A main determinant of strength of want is stated in Axiom 3.3.2 (The strength of P's want of X is directly proportional to the amount of increment in positive or decrement in negative value that P believes will occur when X is attained). From this, two corollaries about change in strength of wants may be derived.

Corollary 7.6.1 *Other things equal, P's want of X is strengthened, if the increment in positive value (decrement in negative value) expected by P to result from achieving X is increased.* Proof: This follows directly from Axiom 3.3.2

Corollary 7.6.2 *Other things equal, P's want of X is weakened, if the increment in positive value (decrement in negative value) expected by P to result from achieving X is decreased.* Proof: This follow from Axiom 3.3.2

Note 7.6.3 Another determinant of strength of want refers to the amount of exertion required to achieve the goal, and is expressed in Axiom 2.4.8 (P wants to minimize exertion). Two theorems about change may be derived from this axiom and Axiom 3.3.2.

Corollary 7.6.4 *Other things equal, P's want to do A is strengthened, if the expected exertion involved in doing A is decreased.* Proof: This follows from Axiom 2.4.8 and Axiom 3.3.2.

Corollary 7.6.5 *Other things equal, P's want to do A is weakened, if the expected exertion involved in doing A is increased.* Proof: This follows from Axiom 2.4.8 and Axiom 3.3.2.

Note 7.6.6 Corollaries 7.6.4 and 7.6.5 are also valid in the special case where the goal is to maximize exertion (e.g., because it is believed to be healthy). If the expected exertion involved in doing A is increased, the want to do A is weakened, because P wants to minimize exertion, but it is also strengthened, because P wants to maximize exertion. The outcome depends on the relative strengths of these two conflicting wants.

7.7 Changes in Strength of Beliefs

Note 7.7.0 A main determinant of strength of belief is stated in Axiom 3.5.1 (The strength of P's belief X, is directly proportional to P's estimate of the likelihood that X is the case). From this four corollaries about change in strength of beliefs may be derived.

Corollary 7.7.1 *P's belief that A leads to G is strengthened, if, and only if, the likelihood, for P, that A leads to G is increased.*   Proof: This follows from Axiom 3.5.1.

Corollary 7.7.2 *P's belief that A leads to G is weakened, if, and only if, the likelihood, for P, that A leads to G is decreased.*   Proof: This follows from Axiom 3.5.1.

Corollary 7.7.3 *P's belief that P can perform A is strengthened, if, and only if, the likelihood, for P, that P can perform A is increased.*   Proof: This follows from Axiom 3.5.1.

Corollary 7.7.4 *P's belief that P can perform A is weakened, if, and only if, the likelihood, for P, that P can perform A is decreased.*   Proof: This follows from Axiom 3.5.1.

Note 7.7.5 The eight corollaries (7.6.1, 7.6.2, 7.6.4, 7.6.5, 7.7.1, 7.7.2, 7.7.3, 7.7.4) state how changes in what is expected are necessary and sufficient for changes in wants and beliefs. The basic condition for the occurrence of such changes is expressed in Axiom 1.5.15 (A person's awareness of the future consists of extrapolations from that person's awareness of trends in the past). In order to change what is expected, the person must be given credible information supporting such a change. "Credible" of course means that the information is believed. Such information may take the form of either direct experiences, or indirect information, either oral or written. In what follows, 13 propositions about change in beliefs are presented. They are slightly modified versions of theorems in my revised formalization of Bandura's theory of self-efficacy (Smedslund, 1982c). The original theorem number is indicated in parentheses.

Corollary 7.7.6 (10) *P's belief that P can do A is strengthened by P's trying to do and succeeding in doing A, and is weakened by P's trying to do and failing to do A, when the strength of the initial belief involved is less than maximal and more than minimal.* Proof: This follows directly from Axiom 1.5.15.

Corollary 7.7.7 (11) *If P believes that A leads to X, and, if P does A and X does not occur, and no other beliefs intervene, then P's belief that A leads to X is weakened.* Proof: This follows directly from Axiom 1.5.15.

Corollary 7.7.8 (12) *If P believes that A leads to X, and, if P tries to do A and fails, and no other beliefs intervene, then P's belief that A leads to X is unchanged.* Proof: This follows directly from Axiom 1.5.15.

Theorem 7.7.9 (19) *Other things equal, P's belief that P can do A is strengthened more by P doing A than by P imagining doing A.* Proof: It is possible to imagine what is not the case. Because P is aware of this, imagining doing A cannot strengthen P's belief that he or she can do A, as much as actually doing A.

Theorem 7.7.10 (20) *If P watches O try to do A and if O succeeds, and if P believes that O is equal or inferior to P in ability to do A, and if P believes that no other circumstances intervene, then P's belief that P can do A is strengthened.* Proof: Because P believes that P is equal or superior in ability to O, in doing A, it follows directly that if O succeeds in doing A, then anyone who is equal or superior in ability to O in doing A will also succeed. Hence, P's belief that P can do A is strengthened.

Theorem 7.7.11 (21) *If P watches O try to do A and if O succeeds, and if P believes P is inferior in ability to O in doing A, and if P believes that the difficulty of A is unchanged, and if no other circumstances intervene, then P's belief that P can do A is not strengthened.* Proof: Because P believes that P is inferior in ability to O, in doing A, nothing can be inferred from what is observed about the outcome of P trying to do A. Hence, P's belief is not strengthened.

Theorem 7.7.12 (22) *Other things equal, if P believes that P is equal or superior in ability to O when it comes to doing A, then P's belief that P can do A is strengthened more by watching O try to do A and succeed, than by watching O try to do A with unknown or ambiguous outcome.* Proof: If P believes that P is equal or superior to O in ability to do A, and O succeeds in doing A, then it follows from Theorem 7.7.10 that P's belief that P can do A is strengthened. If, on the other hand, O's trying to do A has unknown or ambiguous outcome, it can have no definite effect on P's belief. Hence, P's belief that P can do A is not strengthened, and from this the theorem follows.

Theorem 7.7.13 (23) *Other things equal, P's belief that P can do A is strengthened more by watching many persons, unknown to P, succeed in doing A, than by watching only one of these persons succeed in doing A.*
Proof: Because the observed persons are unknown to P, P can only assume that they vary in ability to do A. But this means that the more persons that succeed in doing A, the lower the required minimal ability must be, and the more likely it is that P also can perform A.

Theorem 7.7.14 (24) *Other things equal, and if no other circumstances intervene, P's belief that P can do A is strengthened more by doing A than by being told by O that P can do A.*   Proof: One can be told things which are not true. Because P is aware of this possibility, being told cannot strengthen P's belief that P can do A as much as actually doing it.

Theorem 7.7.15 (29) *If P does A and P believes P succeeded only because P was lucky or aided, then P's belief that P can do A in the future will, other things equal, be strengthened less than if P believes P was neither lucky nor aided.*   Proof: If being "lucky" means to P that achievement was brought about by a combination of random factors, then there is, for P, no predictability for future performance. Hence, the outcome cannot strengthen P's belief that P can do A in the future. Being "aided" without contributing to the result oneself, also means no predictability for future performance in situations without aid. Hence, the outcome cannot strengthen P's belief that P can do A. On the other hand, if P does A without attributing his or her success to circumstances such as luck or aid, then, according to Corollary 7.7.6, P's belief that P can do A is strengthened.

Theorem 7.7.16 (30) *If P tries to do A and fails, and if P believes P failed only because of low ability, then P's belief that P can do A will, other things equal, be weakened more than if P believes it was unusual circumstances only that led to the failure.*   Proof: If P tries to do A and fails, then, according to Corollary 7.7.6, P's belief that P can do A is weakened. But, if the failure is attributed to unusual circumstances only, the failure can have no bearing on performance in usual circumstances. Hence, the belief that P can do A is not weakened. From this the theorem follows.

Theorem 7.7.17 (31) *Other things equal, P's belief that P can do A is strengthened more if P performs effortlessly than if P performs with great effort.*
Proof: According to Axiom 2.3.5, the degree of exertion of P in doing A is inversely proportional to the size of the positive difference between the ability of P to do A

and the difficulty of doing A. Hence, the greater effort P must expend to perform the task, the smaller is the positive difference between the ability of P and the difficulty of the task. But, according to Axiom 2.3.3, P can do A, if, and only if, P's ability to do A is greater than the difficulty of doing A. Hence, the more effort P must use, the higher the likelihood that P will fail. P knows this, and, hence, succeeding in doing A does not strengthen P's belief as much as when he or she performs effortlessly, and, the difference between the ability and difficulty must be large.

Theorem 7.7.18 (32) *Other things equal, if P tries to do A and succeeds, then P's belief that P can do A is strengthened more if P initially regarded A as a very difficult task, than if P initially regarded A as a very easy task.*
Proof: A very easy task means a very high subjective likelihood of success. One actual success, therefore, only confirms an already strong belief, and the subjective likelihood of success cannot be raised very much, given the constraining upper limit of 1.00. On the other hand, a very difficult task means a very low subjective likelihood of success. One actual success, therefore, contradicts a strong belief in failure, and the subjective likelihood of success can rise freely because it is far from the constraining upper limit. Hence, the theorem is proved.

Note 7.7.19 Theorem 33 in Smedslund (1978a) and (1982c) is identical to Axiom 1.5.15 here.

Note 7.7.20 Theorem 34 (Smedslund 1978a, 1982c) is merely an application of Corollary 7.7.3 to the special case of generalizing from a more to a less protected condition. Similarly, Theorem 35 (Smedslund, 1978a, 1982c) is equivalent to Theorem 23 (here Theorem 7.7.13), but applied to contexts rather than persons. The proofs have the same structure. Theorem 36 (The more credible O is to P, the more P will be influenced in P's beliefs about what P can do, by what O tells him or her.) merely formulates a direct consequence of what is meant by *credibility*.

7.8 Changes in Strength of Feelings

Note 7.8.0 Because feelings are not conceptually independent of wants and beliefs, changes in strength of feelings are derivative of changes in strength of wants and beliefs. Even so, formulations directly concerning feelings may be helpful for particular purposes. The main determinants of strength of feeling are stated in Axiom 4.3.0. (The strength of a feeling is equal to the product of the strength of the want and the strength of the belief, whose relationship constitutes the feeling.)

Corollary 7.8.1 *The strength of P's feeling changes, if, and only if, either the strength of the constituent want(s) changes, with the strength of the* *constituent belief(s) remaining constant, or the strength of the constituent belief(s) changes, with the strength of the constituent want(s) remaining constant, or both the strength of the constituent want(s) and the strength of the constituent belief(s) change, but in such a way that these changes do not exactly compensate each other.*   Proof: This follows directly from Axiom 4.3.0.

Note 7.8.2 Corollary 7.8.1 states that, in order for the strength of a feeling to change, the changes in the strengths of the wants and the beliefs involved must not exactly compensate each other. Example: The want to escape a danger diminishes, hence diminishing the fear, but the likelihood of the feared event increases, hence increasing the fear. If the decrement and increment are exactly equal, the outcome is an unchanged degree of fear, even though both the constituent want and the constituent belief has changed.

Note 7.8.3 The preceding means that changing the wants and/or the beliefs exhausts the possibilities for changing feelings. If someone takes valium to reduce fear, and if there is no change in the relevant beliefs, then it follows that the valium must have changed (weakened) the want of the person to escape the danger. Conversely, if there is no change in the person's want to escape the danger, then the valium must have changed the person's estimate of the likelihood that what is feared will actually happen. The present analysis does not allow for the possibility that valium can reduce fear, and not change the constituent want(s) and/or the constituent belief(s) of the person.

Note 7.8.4 As has been pointed out earlier, amount and kind of physiological arousal is a symptom of feeling, but not a criterion. In particular, the arousal does not indicate *what* feeling is involved. For example, if a person has a high degree of arousal, but does not have any want to escape a painful event and does not believe that such an event is imminent, then the arousal cannot be indicative of fear. In practice, high arousal may often be taken as a symptom that the person harbors a strong feeling. However, *what* this feeling is, must be decided by considering what wants and beliefs are involved. Also, because arousal is a symptom and not a criterion, it is conceivable that a person can be in a state of strong arousal for some *other* reason than having a feeling. It is also conceivable that a person can have a strong feeling, even without being strongly aroused physiologically.

7.9 *Changes in Strength of Specific Feelings*

Note 7.9.0 In the present system all changes in feeling are reduced to changes in strength of specific feelings. For example, a change from being afraid to being angry is conceptualized as a decrease in the strength of fear and a concomitant increase in the strength of anger.

Although nothing more can be said generally about changing the strength of feelings, it is possible to formulate a set of corollaries, two for each of the ten specific feelings included in the present system. One corollary for each feeling states how that feeling is created and the other states how the feeling is extinguished. They summarize the explanations that are given in everyday life of the waxing and waning of feelings.

Corollary 7.9.1 *If P begins to believe that one of P's wants is being, or is going to be, fulfilled, then P begins to feel happy.* Proof: This follows directly from Axiom 4.5.1.

Note 7.9.2 This corollary can also incorporate the case where P is given something that is not wanted in advance, but that is liked. This makes P want to retain it, and the fulfillment of this want also creates happiness.

Corollary 7.9.3 *If P begins to believe that one of P's wants is not going to be fulfilled, then P begins to feel unhappy.* Proof: This follows directly from Axiom 4.5.1.

Note 7.9.4 This corollary also incorporates the case where P gets something that P has not wanted to avoid in advance, but that is disliked. This makes P want to avoid it, and the lack of fulfillment of this want means feeling unhappy.

Corollary 7.9.5 *If P comes to believe that P cannot act toward any of P's goals, and that P cannot leave for some time, then P becomes bored.* Proof: This follows directly from Axiom 4.6.1.

Corollary 7.9.6 *If P is bored, and P comes to believe that P can act toward one of P's goals, then P ceases to be bored.* Proof: This follows directly from Axiom 4.6.1.

Corollary 7.9.7 *If P comes to believe that at least one person whom P cares for, has intentionally or through neglect, been treated without respect by O, and P has not forgiven O, then P becomes angry at O.* Proof: This follows directly from Axiom 4.6.4.

Corollary 7.9.8 *If P is angry at O, and, then, comes to believe that no person P cares for, has intentionally or through neglect, been treated without respect by O, then P ceases to be angry at O.* Proof: This follows directly from Axiom 4.6.4.

Note 7.9.9 Corollary 7.9.8 does not describe the only way in which P can cease to be angry at O. P can also cease to be angry through *forgiving* O. The concept of forgiving has been analyzed in a preliminary way in Smedslund (1991a); (P forgives O = df P ceases to believe that O does not respect P). This definition of forgiving emphasizes the current situation, rather than redefining the past. In the past there may have been occasion for anger, but today there is none and therefore, the past is shelved. Forgiving involves a shelving of the past.

Corollary 7.9.10 *If P comes to believe that, regardless of what P does, there is a definite likelihood that P will be harmed, then P becomes afraid.* Proof: This follows directly from Axiom 4.6.11.

Corollary 7.9.11 *If P is afraid, and then comes to believe that it is unlikely that P will be harmed, then P will cease to be afraid.*   Proof: This follows directly from Axiom 4.6.11.

Corollary 7.9.12 *If P comes to believe that P has done something that P ought not to have done, either because it is not regarded as seemly, or because it was done incompetently, then P becomes ashamed.*   Proof: This follows directly from Axiom 4.6.17.

Corollary 7.9.13 *If P is ashamed, and then comes to believe that P has not done anything that P ought not to have done, either because it is regarded as unseemly, or because it was done incompetently, then P ceases to be ashamed.*   Proof: This follows directly from Axiom 4.6.17.

Corollary 7.9.14 *If P comes to believe that P has done something wrong to O, then P begins to feel guilty.*   Proof: This follows directly from Axiom 4.6.21.

Corollary 7.9.15 *If P is feeling guilty toward O, and then comes to believe that P has not done anything wrong to O, then P ceases to feel guilty.* Proof: This follows directly from Axiom 4.6.21.

Note 7.9.16 Corollary 7.9.15 does not describe the only way in which a person may cease to feel guilty. Another way is through achieving forgiveness (cf. Notes 4.6.26 and 7.9.9; Smedslund, 1991a).

Corollary 7.9.17 *If P comes to believe that something P wants has become irrevocably lost, then P will become sad.*   Proof: This follows directly from Definition 4.6.28.

Corollary 7.9.18 *If P is sad about losing something, and, then, comes to believe that this something is not, after all, irrevocably lost, then P will cease to be sad.*   Proof: This follows directly from Axiom 4.6.28.

Corollary 7.9.19 *If P comes to believe that P's lot in life can never be improved in the way P wants it to be, or P can never become the sort of person P wants to be, then P will become depressed.* Proof: This follows directly from Axiom 4.6.32.

Corollary 7.9.20 *If P is depressed, and then comes to believe that P's lot in life can be improved in the way P wants it, and/or that P can become the sort of person P wants to be, then P will cease to be depressed.* Proof: This follows directly from Axiom 4.6.32.

Corollary 7.9.21 *If P begins to want to have what O has and/or to want O not to have it, then P becomes envious of O.* Proof: This follows directly from Axiom 4.6.35.

Corollary 7.9.22 *If P is envious of O, and then ceases to want to have what O has and/or ceases to want O not to have what O has, then P ceases to be envious of O.* Proof: This follows directly from Axiom 4.6.35.

Corollary 7.9.23 *If P comes to believe that something may not be what it appears to be, and that this appearance is intentional, then P becomes suspicious.* Proof: This follows directly from Axiom 4.6.39.

Corollary 7.9.24 *If P is suspicious about something, and then comes to believe that this something is what it appears to be, and/or that the discrepancy is unintentional, then P ceases to be suspicious.* Proof: This follows directly from Axiom 4.6.39.

Corollary 7.9.25 *If P comes into contact with X, and contact with X is incompatible with P's moral and/or esthetic and/or hygienic standards, then P becomes disgusted.* Proof: This follows directly from Axiom 4.6.42.

Corollary 7.9.26 *If P is disgusted by being in contact with X, and then P comes to believe that being in contact with X is compatible with P's moral, esthetic, and hygienic standards or P ceases to be in contact with X, then P ceases to be disgusted.* Proof: This follows directly from Axiom 4.6.42.

Note 7.9.27 Changes in personal activity may be subdivided into first-order changes, which reflect changes in context, and second-order changes, which reflect changes in the person's disposition. First-order changes are reversible and second-order changes are irreversible. Second-order changes include discrimination between situations, differentiation between acts, transition from the unreflective to the reflective mode. The basic principle of learning is that a person's awareness of the future is based on extrapolations from the past as it was experienced by that person. Under special conditions, there is a search for differentiating cues or for common factors. Changes in acting depend systematically on changes in can and try. Changes in can depend on changes in the ability of the person and the difficulty of the task, and changes in try depend on changes in want, likelihood of achieving the outcome, and likelihood of being able to carry out the act involved. Changes in feelings occur as a function of changes in the constituent wants and beliefs.

7.10 Epilogue

The system presented here is basically unchanged in content from the first version (Smedslund, 1988a). It may be taken to reflect some of the basic design features of natural language, as they apply to the description of personal activity. In order to make sense, we *must* conform to these invariant structures when we talk and think about psychology.

The propositions and proofs are written in a style that differs from the way we talk in everyday life. In a recent study (Smedslund, 1997c) native speakers of Arabic, Ewe, Norwegian, Tamil, Turkish,and Vietnamese agreed that propositions of psychologic are unnatural, stilted, and cognitively demanding. Yet, they also agreed that the propositions are meaningful and tend to be necessarily true. Can the present explication of psychological common sense function as a useful analytic instrument? Can it predict outcomes from given premises, and can it be helpful in revealing faulty instruments and methods on the basis of failing predictions? The answer can only come from future work.

However, the emergence of psychologic forces the psychologist to upgrade the methical standards for empirical and theoretical research. Empirical work must not be pseudo-empirical, that is, it must not investigate logically necessary relationships. Theoretical work must conform to higher standards of preciseness. One must be able to decide what follows and does not follow from given propositions.

What can this, admittedly dry and technical presentation, give to the student who is fascinated by the richness and mysteries of psychological phenomena? Having worked as a clinical psychologist for over two decades, I understand and share that fascination. Yet, I am also concerned about the slow and uncertain progress of our discipline and profession over the last century. We are flooded by research data and raw clinical experience, but the irreversibility of psychological processes, and the corresponding uniqueness of persons and circumstances, prevents us from formulating any general empirical laws. Looking for alternate paths ahead, I think we must pause and consider the endlessly repeated, but relatively limited, set of words we use to describe psychological phenomena. These words are not a haphazard collection, but form a system of meanings. That system is explicated in psychologic. Will this help?

Appendix A :

Primitive Terms

1.0.1 *Person*

1.1.0 *Aware*

1.2.1 *Act (Do)*

1.3.0 *Right*

1.3.1 *Wrong*

1.4.10 *Talk (Say)*

1.5.5 *When*

1.5.6 *After*

1.5.7 *Before*

1.5.8 *Now*

2.2.1 *Can*

2.2.2 *Try*

2.3.0 *Ability*

2.3.1 *Difficulty*

2.4.1 *Good*

2.4.2 *Bad*

2.4.3 *Feel*

2.4.6 *Exertion*

3.1.1 *Want*

3.3.0 *Strength*

3.4.0 *Belief*

5.3.0 *Understand*

Appendix B:

Definitions

3.4.9 *Reflective Believing*

3.4.13 *Unreflective Believing*

3.5.5 *Conflict of Beliefs*

4.2.1 *Reflective Feeling*

4.2.2 *Unreflective Feeling*

4.3.8 *Conflict of Feelings*

5.1.1 *Respect*

5.1.2 *Treat with Respect*

5.2.1 *Care*

5.2.7 *Like*

5.4.0 *Control*

5.4.6 *Own-Control*

5.4.8 *Other-Control*

5.5.5 *Trust*

6.1.0 *Self-Respect*

6.1.1 *Treat Self With Respect*

6.2.0 *Self-Care*

6.2.9 *Self-Like*

6.4.1 *Self-Control*

6.5.2 *Self-Trust*

7.1.0 *First-Order Change*

7.1.2 *Second-Order Change*

Appendix C:

Axioms

Axiom 1.1.3 *P is aware of X, if, and only if, X exists FOR P*

Axiom 1.1.14 *P is conscious, if, and only if, P is in a state in which P is aware of something*

Axiom 1.2.4 *Acting is intentional*

Axiom 1.2.16 *A person's acting tends to be completely integrated (unitary)*

Axiom 1.3.4 *A person is held responsible for his or her acts by everyone involved*

Axiom 1.3.9 *P wants to do what P believes is right and wants not to do what P believes is wrong*

Axiom 1.3.11 *P wants everyone to accept what P believes is right and to reject what P believes is wrong*

Axiom 1.4.6 *P can be reflectively aware if, and only if, P is a person*

Axiom 1.4.11 *P can talk about what P is reflectively aware of, and only that*

Axiom 1.4.32 *P's description of what P is reflectively aware of is correct, to the extent that P regards it as correct*

Axiom 1.4.39 *The unreflective is not differentiated according to viewpoints*

Axiom 1.5.2 *Learning (the impact of experience) is irreversible*

Axiom 1.5.15 *P's awareness of the future consists of extrapolations from P's awareness of trends in the past*

Axiom 2.0.1 *A conscious person is continuously acting*

Axiom 2.2.3 *P does A, if, and only if, P can do A, and P tries to do A*

Axiom 2.3.3 *P can do A, if, and only if, P's ability to do A is greater than the difficulty of A*

Axiom 2.3.5 *The degree of exertion of P in doing A is inversely proportional to the size of the positive difference between the ability of P to do A and the difficulty of doing A*

Axiom 2.4.8 *P wants to minimize exertion*

Axiom 2.4.12 *P tries to maximize expected utility*

Axiom 3.1.3 *P wants X, if, and only if, other things equal, P prefers X to not-X*

Axiom 3.2.1 *P wants to feel good and wants to avoid feeling bad*

Axiom 3.2.9 *A want is fulfilled, if, and only if, and to the extent that, the expected increment in positive or decrement in negative value occurs*

Axiom 3.2.10 *A want is frustrated, if, and only if, and to the extent that, the expected increment in positive or decrement in negative value does not occur*

Axiom 3.2.13 *If two positive or two negative values, p1 and p2, occur at the same time, they combine in such a way that p1 & p2 > p1, and p1 & p2 > p2. If a positive (p1) and a negative (p2) value occur at the same time, they combine in such a way that p1 & p2 < p1, and p1 & p2 > p2*

Axiom 3.3.2 *The strength of P's want of X is directly proportional to the amount of increment in positive or decrement in negative value that P believes will occur when X is attained*

Axiom 3.3.5 *P's want A is stronger than P's want B, if, and only if, when A and B are in conflict, and no other factors intervene, P tries to act according to A and not according to B*

Axiom 3.4.2 *P believes X, if, and only if, for P, X is the case*

Axiom 3.5.1 *The strength of P's belief X is directly proportional to P's estimate of the likelihood that X is the case*

Axiom 3.5.4 *P's belief A is stronger than P's belief B, if, and only if, when A and B are in conflict, and no other factors intervene, P tries to act according to A and not according to B*

Axiom 3.6.2 *P wants to believe what is the case*

Axiom 3.7.1 *P reflectively believes that P exists and that other persons exist*

Axiom 3.7.5 *Every person reflectively wants to continue to exist*

Axiom 3.7.12 *If everyone takes a psychological proposition X to be self-evident, then everyone believes that everyone else takes X to be self-evident, everyone believes that everyone else believes that everyone else takes X to be self-evident, everyone believes that everyone else believes that everyone else believes that everyone else takes X to be self-evident, and so on.*

Axiom 4.1.1 *P's feeling follows from P's awareness of the relationship between P's wants and P's beliefs*

Axiom 4.3.0 *The strength of a feeling is equal to the product of the strength of the want and the strength of the belief, whose relationship constitutes the feeling*

Axiom 4.4.5 *The sum of the strengths of P's feelings at a given moment has an upper limit equal to the maximum possible strength of any single feeling at that moment*

Axiom 4.5.1 *P is happy, if, and only if, and to the extent that, P believes that at least one of P's wants are, or is going to be, fulfilled*

Axiom 4.6.1 *P is bored, if, and only if, P believes that P cannot act toward any of P's goals, and cannot leave the situation for some time*

Axiom 4.6.4 *P is angry at O, if, and only if, P believes that at least one person whom P cares for has, intentionally or through neglect, been treated without respect by O, and P has not forgiven O*

Axiom 4.6.11 *P is afraid, if, and only if, P believes that, regardless of what P does, there is a definite possibility that P will be harmed*

Axiom 4.6.17 *P feels ashamed, if, and only if, P believes that P has done something which P ought not to have done, either because it is regarded as unseemly, or because it was done incompetently*

Axiom 4.6.21 *P feels guilt toward O, if, and only if, P believes that P has done something wrong to O and has not been forgiven*

Axiom 4.6.28 *P is sad, if, and only if, P believes that something P wants has become irrevocably lost*

Axiom 4.6.32 *P is depressed, if, and only if, P believes that P's lot can never be improved in the way P wants it to be, and/or P can never become the sort of person P wants to be*

Axiom 4.6.35 *P is envious of O, if, and only if, P wants to have something that P believes O has, and/or wants O not to have it*

Axiom 4.6.39 *P is suspicious, if, and only if, P believes that something may not be what it appears to be, and that this discrepancy is intentional*

Axiom 4.6.42 *P is disgusted with X, if, and only if, P is in contact with X, and this is incompatible with P's moral and/or esthetic and/or hygienic standards*

Axiom 5.1.17 *For every P, there exists at least one O, such that P respects O, and P wants O to respect P*

Axiom 5.2.10 *Every person wants to care for someone*

Axiom 5.3.1 *P understands what O means by saying or doing A, if, and only if, P and O agree as to what, for O, is equivalent to A, implied by A, contradicted by A, and irrelevant to A*

Axiom 5.3.3 *P understands why O does A, if, and only if, P and O agree about which wants and beliefs of O are involved in O doing A*

Axiom 5.3.15 *All understanding depends on relevant preunderstanding*

Axiom 5.5.2 *P believes that O can harm P*

Axiom 6.0.6 *P*O is a consensually self-evident interpersonal proposition, if, and only if, P*P is a consensually self-evident intrapersonal proposition*

Axiom 6.2.12 *P wants to care for P*

Axiom 6.5.1 *P believes that P can harm P*

Appendix D:

Presentations, Critiques, and Replies Concerning or Related to Psychologic

So much is written about the various topics of common sense psychology that the task of giving references is entirely unmanageable. However, I have found it useful to assemble the published presentations, critiques, and replies directly concerned with the project of psychologic. They are, with a few exceptions, not referred to in the text, since they concern general metatheoretical issues not treated in the present volume.

Bandura, A. (1978). On distinguishing between logical and empirical verification. A comment on Smedslund. *Scandinavian Journal of Psychology, 19*, 97–99.

Cushman, P. (1991). Psychologic or psychological esperanto? *Psychological Inquiry, 2*, 339–342.

Davis, K. E. (1991). Two cheers for psychologic—and three reservations. *Psychological Inquiry, 2*, 343–345.

De Gelder, B. (1987). Commonsense mentalism and psychological theory. In F. van Holthoon & D. R. Olson, (Eds.), *Common sense: The foundations for social science* (pp. 277–296). Lanham, MD: University Press of America.

Eilan, N. (1992). The a priori and the empirical in theories of emotion: Smedslund's "conceptual analysis" of emotion. *Cognition and Emotion, 6*, 457–466.

Fiske, D. W. (1991). Common sense is just one strategy. *Psychological Inquiry, 2*, 345–346.

Frijda, N. H. (1992). The empirical status of the laws of emotion. *Cognition and Emotion, 6*, 467–477.

Goddard, C. & Wierzbicka, A. (Eds.). (1994). *Semantic and lexical universals*, Amsterdam: John Benjamins.

Howard, G. S. (1991). Stop the presses! I think my research is pseudoempirical. *Psychological Inquiry, 2*, 347–350.

van Ijzendoorn, M. H. (1995). Psycho-Logic: The blind and context-free search for noncontingent "truth". *Human Development, 38*, 170–173.

Jones, A. J. I. (1980). Psychology and "ordinary language"—A critique of Smedslund. *Scandinavian Journal of Psychology, 21*, 225–229.

Lazarus, R. S. (1991). *Emotion and adaptation.* New York: Oxford University Press.

Lewis, D. (1972). Psychophysical and theoretical identifications. *Australian Journal of Philosophy, 50*, 249–258.

Lock, A. (1981). Indigenous psychology and human nature: A psychological perspective. In P. Heelas & A. Lock (Eds.), *Indigenous Psychologies: The Anthropology of the Self.* London: Academic Press.

McCall, R. B. (1994). Commentary. *Human Development, 37,* 293–298.

Ossorio, P. G. (1991). Naive baseball theory. *Psychological Inquiry, 2,* 352–355.

Overton, W. F. (1991). Narratives and observations in contemporary scientific psychology. *Psychological Inquiry, 2,* 356–357.

Parrott, W. G., & Harre, R. (1991). Smedslundian suburbs in the city of language: The case of embarrassment. *Psychological Inquiry, 2,* 358–361.

Rosenhan, D. L. (1991). Pseudoempiricism: who owns the right to scientific reality? *Psychological Inquiry, 2,* 361–363.

Shotter, J. (1991). Measuring blindly and speculating loosely: but is a "psychologic" the answer? *Psychological Inquiry, 2,* 363–366.

Shotter, J. (1994). Is there a logic in common sense? The scope and limits of Jan Smedslund's "geometric" psychologic. In J. Siegfried (Ed.), *The status of common sense in psychology* (pp.149–168). Norwood, NJ: Ablex.

Shotter, J., & Burton, M. (1983). Common sense accounts of human action: The descriptive formulations of Heider, Smedslund, and Ossorio. In L. Wheeler (Ed.), *Review of personality and social psychology*: Vol.4. Beverly Hills, CA: Sage.

Shweder, R. A. (1991). On pseudoempiricism, pseudodeductionism, and common sense. *Psychological Inquiry, 2,* 366–371.

Shweder, R. A. (1993). Everything you ever wanted to know about cognitive appraisal theory without being conscious of it. (Book review essay on Lazarus' Emotion and Adaptation). *Psychological Inquiry, 4,* 322–326.

Siegfried, J. (1994). Commonsense language and the limits of theory construction in psychology. In J. Siegfried (Ed.), *The status of common sense in psychology* (pp.3–34), Norwood, NJ: Ablex.

Sjoberg, L. (1982). Logical versus psychological necessity: A discussion of the role of common sense in psychological theory. *Scandinavian Journal of Psychology, 23,* 65–78.

Smedslund, J. (1970). Circular relation between understanding and logic. *Scandinavian Journal of Psychology, 11,* 217–219.

Smedslund, J. (1978a). Bandura's theory of self-efficacy: A set of common sense theorems. *Scandinavian Journal of Psychology, 19,* 1–14.

Smedslund, J. (1978b). Some psychological theories are not empirical: Reply to Bandura. *Scandinavian Journal of Psychology, 19,* 101–102.

Smedslund, J. (1979). Between the analytic and the arbitrary: A case study of psychological research. *Scandinavian Journal of Psychology, 20,* 1–12.

Smedslund, J. (1980a). Analyzing the primary code: From empiricism to apriorism. In D. R. Olson (Ed.), *The social foundations of language and thought: Essays in honor of Jerome S. Bruner* (pp. 47–73), New York: Norton.

Smedslund, J. (1980b). From ordinary to scientific language: Reply to Jones. *Scandinavian Journal of Psychology, 21,* 231–233.

Smedslund, J. (1981). The logic of psychological treatment. *Scandinavian Journal of Psychology, 22,* 65–77.

Smedslund, J. (1982a). Common sense as psychosocial reality: A reply to Sjoberg. *Scandinavian Journal of Psychology, 23,* 79–82.

Smedslund, J. (1982b). Seven common sense rules of psychological treatment. *Journal of the Norwegian Psychological Association, 19,* 441–449.

Smedslund, J. (1982c). Revising explications of common sense through dialogue: Thirty-six psychological theorems. *Scandinavian Journal of Psychology, 23*, 299–305.

Smedslund, J. (1984a). The invisible obvious: Culture in psychology. In K. M. J. Lagerspetz & P. Niemi (Eds.), *Psychology in the 1990's* (pp. 443–452). Amsterdam: Elsevier. Science Publishers.

Smedslund, J. (1984b). What is necessarily true in psychology? In J. R. Royce & L. P. Mos (Eds.), *Annals of theoretical psychology* (Vol. 2, 241–272). New York: Plenum Press.

Smedslund, J. (1984c). Psychology cannot take leave of common sense: Reply to Tennesen, Vollmer, and Wilkes. In J. R. Royce & L. P. Mos (Eds.), *Annals of theoretical psychology*, (Vol. 2, 295–302). New York: Plenum Press.

Smedslund, J. (1985). Necessarily true cultural psychologies. In K. J. Gergen & K. E. Davis (Eds.), *The social construction of the person* (pp.73–87). New York: Springer.

Smedslund, J. (1986a). The explication of psychological common sense: Implications for the science of psychology. In R. Barcan Marcus, G. J. W. Dorn, & P. Weingartner (Eds.), *Logic, methodology and philosophy of science* (Vol. 7, pp. 481–494). Amsterdam: Elsevier.

Smedslund, J. (1986b). How stable is common sense psychology and can it be transcended? Reply to Valsiner. *Scandinavian Journal of Psychology, 27*, 91–94.

Smedslund, J. (1987a). Das Beschreiben von Beschreibungen, Erklaeren von Erklaerungen und Vorhersagen von Vorhersagen: Paradigmatische Faelle fuer die Psychologie. In J. Brandtstaedter (Ed.) *Struktur und Erfahrung in der psychologischen Forschung* (pp. 159–168). Berlin: de Gruyter.

Smedslund, J. (1987b). The epistemic status of interitem correlations in Eysenck's Personality Questionnaire: The a priori versus the empirical in psychological data. *Scandinavian Journal of Psychology, 28*, 42–55.

Smedslund, J. (1987c). Ebbinghaus the illusionist: How psychology came to look like an experimental science. In *Passauer Schriften zur Psychologiegeschichte, 5*, Ebbinghaus–Studien 2 (pp. 225–239). Passau: Passavia Universitaetsverlag.

Smedslund, J. (1988a). *Psycho-Logic.* New York: Springer-Verlag.

Smedslund, J. (1988b). Fritz Heider misinterpreted. *Contemporary Psychology, 33*,(3), 275.

Smedslund, J. (1988c). What is measured by a psychological measure? *Scandinavian Journal of Psychology, 29*, 148–151.

Smedslund, J. (1989). The hall of mirrors in psychological theorizing. In I. A. Bjørgen (Ed.), *Basic issues in psychology. A Scandinavian contribution* (pp. 255–261). London: Sigma.

Smedslund, J. (1990a). Psychology and psychologic: Characterization of the difference. In K. J. Gergen & G. R. Semin (Eds.), *Everyday understanding. Social and scientific implications* (pp. 45–65). London: Sage.

Smedslund, J. (1990b). A critique of Tversky & Kahneman's distinction between fallacy and misunderstanding. *Scandinavian Journal of Psychology, 31*, 110–120.

Smedslund, J. (1991a). The psychologic of forgiving. *Scandinavian Journal of Psychology, 32*, 164–176.

Smedslund, J. (1991b). What is psychologic? In W. J. Baker, R. van Hezewijk, M. E. Hyland, & S. Terwee (Eds.), *Recent advances in theoretical psychology* (Vol. 2, pp. 453–457). New York: Springer-Verlag.

Smedslund, J. (1991c). The pseudoempirical in psychology and the case for psychologic. *Psychological Inquiry, 2*, 325–338.

Smedslund, J. (1991d). Psychologic: A technical language for psychology. *Psychological Inquiry, 2*, 376–382.

Smedslund, J. (1992). Are Frijda's "Laws of emotion" empirical? *Cognition and Emotion*, *6*, 435–456.

Smedslund, J. (1993). How shall the concept of anger be defined? *Theory and Psychology*, *3*, 5–33.

Smedslund, J. (1994a). Nonempirical and empirical components in the hypotheses of five social psychological experiments. *Scandinavian Journal of Psychology*, *35*, 1–15.

Smedslund, J. (1994b). What kind of propositions are set forth in developmental research? Five case studies. *Human Development*, *37*, 259–276.

Smedslund, J. (1995a). The psycho-logic of action. Reply to Vollmer. *Scandinavian Journal of Psychology*, *36*, 232–234.

Smedslund, J. (1995b). Psychologic: Common sense, and the pseudoempirical. In J. Smith, R. Harre, & L. Van Langenhove (Eds.), *Rethinking psychology* (pp. 196–206). London: Sage.

Smedslund, J. (1995c). Auxiliary versus theoretical hypotheses and ordinary versus scientific language. *Human Development*, *38*, 174–178.

Smedslund, J. (1997a). The ambiguity of covariation: A conceptual note. *Scandinavian Journal of Psychology*, *38*, 32–35.

Smedslund, J. (1997b). The forgotten variable of understanding. *Cahiers de Psychologie Cognitive/Current Psychology of Cognition*, *16*, 217–221.

Smedslund, J. (1997). Is the psychologic of trust universal? In R. Dirven & S. Niemeier (Eds.), *The language of emotions* (pp. 3–13). Amsterdam: Benjamins.

Smith, L. (1993). *Necessary knowledge*. Hove, UK: Lawrence Erlbaum Associates.

Tennesen, H. (1984). What is remarkable in psychology? In J. R. Royce & L. P. Mos (Eds.), *Annals of theoretical psychology* (Vol. 2, pp. 273–278).

Valsiner, J. (1985). Common sense and psychological theories: The historical nature of logical necessity. *Scandinavian Journal of Psychology*, *26*, 97–109.

Vollmer, F. (1984). On the limitations of commonsense psychology. In J. R. Royce & L. P. Mos (Eds.), *Annals of theoretical psychology* (Vol. 2, pp. 279–286).

Vollmer, F. (1994). Remarks on the psycho-logic of action. *Scandinavian Journal of Psychology*, 1994, *35*, 86–90.

Wilkes, K. V. (1984). It ain't necessarily so. In J. R. Royce & L. P. Mos (Eds.), *Annals of theoretical psychology* (Vol. 2, pp.287–294).

Williams, R. N. (1991). The pseudofundamental in psychology: psychologic and psychologism. *Psychological Inquiry*, *2*, 371–374.

Woolfolk, R. L. (1991). Logic, contingency, and psychological knowledge. *Psychological Inquiry*, *2*, 374–375.